BE INFANTS IN EVIL

A NEW PLAY BY BRIAN MARTIN

SAMUELFRENCH-LONDON.CO.UK
SAMUELFRENCH.COM

Be Infants in Evil by Brian Martin received its world premiere at The Mick Lally Theatre, Druid Lane, Galway on the 15ᵗʰ of July 2014.

CAST

PRIEST	Marty Rea
NOLEEN	Marion O'Dwyer
JACINTA	Roxanna Nic Liam
HENRY	Bailey Hayden

PRODUCTION TEAM

DIRECTOR	Oonagh Murphy
DESIGNER	Alyson Cummins
LIGHTING DESIGNER	Stephen Dodd
DRAMATURG	Thomas Conway
PRODUCTION MANAGER	Barry O'Brien
COMPANY STAGE MANAGER	Paula Tierney
DEPUTY STAGE MANAGER	Clare Howe
ASSISTANT STAGE MANAGER	Sophie Flynn
WARDROBE SUPERVISOR	Doreen McKenna
CHIEF LX	Shannon Light
STAGE TECHNICIAN	Frank Commins
MASTER CARPENTER	Gus Dewar
PUBLICIST	Kate Bowe PR
GRAPHIC DESIGN	Bite! Associates

PATRON

Michael D. Higgins, President of Ireland

BOARD

Cathal Goan (Chairman)
Tarlach DeBlacam
Eugene Downes
Donncha O'Connell
Séamus O'Grady
Bride Rosney
Bernadette Murtagh (Company Secretary)

DRUID

ARTISTIC DIRECTOR .... Garry Hynes
GENERAL MANAGER .... Sarah Lynch
PRODUCTION ASSOCIATE .... Craig Flaherty
FINANCIAL CONTROLLER .... Brian Duffy*
FINANCIAL ADMINISTRATOR .... Lisa Nolan*
OFFICE ASSISTANT .... Rory Lorton*

*Part time

DRUID
Flood Street, Galway, Ireland.
T: +353 91 568660
E: info@druid.ie
www.druid.ie

Acknowledgments
Druid is grant aided by the Arts Council of Ireland and gratefully acknowledges the support of NUI Galway

DRUID

"It's not theatre until someone's watching"

At the heart of everything we do is our audience. Our goal is to create electrifying theatre experiences for every person, in every place and every time we perform.

Druid was founded in Galway in 1975 by graduates of the National University of Ireland, Galway, Garry Hynes, Mick Lally (1945 – 2010) and Marie Mullen – the first professional theatre company in Ireland to be based outside Dublin. The company has had two artistic directors: Garry Hynes (1975–91 and 1995 to date) and Maeliosa Stafford (1991–94).

Druid has always seen itself as a theatre for Ireland and since its foundation has been at the forefront of the development of Irish theatre. Touring the length and breadth of Ireland is an essential part of the company's mission and Druid passionately believes that audiences have a right to see first class professional theatre without having to travel long distances outside their own communities. The company has toured to every nook and cranny in Ireland as well as touring to key global centres around the world including UK, America, Canada, Australia, New Zealand and Japan, making Druid one of the best-known Irish theatre companies in the English-speaking world.

Since 1979, the company has had its own theatre on Druid Lane in Galway. The theatre is the birthplace of all the work and continues to serve as a facility for the promotion and development of the arts in Galway. The auditorium was renamed The Mick Lally Theatre in November 2013.

Recent productions include The Colleen Bawn by Dion Boucicault, DruidMurphy plays by Tom Murphy – Conversations on a Homecoming, A Whistle in the Dark and Famine. Big Maggie by John B.Keane, The Silver Tassie by Sean O'Casey, The Cripple of Inishmaan by Martin McDonagh.

Druid consistently brings groundbreaking productions of classic and new dramatic works to the world stage and, as such, has drawn extensively from the Irish dramatic repertoire and has worked with celebrated Irish and international playwrights.

CAST

MARTY REA *(Priest)*

Druid Theatre Company: The Colleen Bawn, DruidMurphy – Three Plays by Tom Murphy (International and National tours).

Other Theatre Includes: An Ideal Husband, My Cousin Rachel, Little Women, Hay Fever, Salomé, The Glass Menagerie, Arcadia (Gate Theatre); The Hanging Gardens, Major Barbara, John Gabriel Borkman, The Rivals, Only An Apple, An Ideal Husband, The Big House, Saved, The Importance of Being Earnest (Abbey Theatre); Improbable Frequency (E59 Street Theatre, New York); Pentecost, Spokesong (The Lyric Theatre, Rough Magic Theatre Co.); Philadelphia, Here I Come!, Hamlet (Irish Times Best Actor Award 2011, Second Age Theatre Co.); Observe the Sons of Ulster Marching Towards the Somme (Livin' Dred Theatre Co. & NOMAD Theatre Network); Smilin' Through (Birmingham Rep.); Philadelphia, Here I Come! (ART NI).

Film & Television: The Devil's Pool (dir. Cecily Brennan, Vico Films); The Man Inside (dir. Rory Bresnihan, Broken Pictures Ltd.); Vingt Minutes (dir. Lois Espana, Case Television).

Radio: BBC Northern Ireland, BBC Radio 4 and RTÉ Radio Drama.

Marty received the Lady Rothermere Scholarship in 1999 and graduated from the Royal Academy of Dramatic Art (RADA) in 2002.

MARION O'DWYER *(Noleen)*

Druid Theatre Company: The Silver Tassie, The Loves of Cass Maguire, Poor Beast in the Rain, Lovers Meeting, The Donahue Sisters.

Other Theatre Includes: An Ideal Husband, A Streetcar Named Desire, A Woman of No Importance, The Speckled People (The Gate); The Government Inspector, Bookworms, The Rivals, Big Love, The Crucible, The Plough and the Stars, Portia Coughlan (The Abbey Theatre); Wonderful Tennessee (The Abbey Theatre & on Broadway); Dancing at Lughnasa (Abbey Theatre & Australian tour); Philadelphia Here I Come! (Lyric Theatre); The Cavalcaders (Decadent); Payback (Bewleys); Shadow of a Gunman (Tricycle Theatre); Molly Sweeney (Bristol Old Vic); Juno and the Paycock (Gaiety Theatre & Chicago Theatre Festival).

Film & Television: Hannah Cohen's Holy Communion, Love Rosie, Covet, Ondine, Agnes Browne, Green, Moone Boy, Love/Hate, The Savage Eye, The Clinic, Poirot, Ballykissangel, The Life of Reilly.

ROXANNA NIC LIAM *(Jacinta)*

Druid Theatre Company: Be Infants in Evil marks Roxanna's debut with Druid.

Other Theatre Includes: The Separation (Pixilated); Translations (English Touring Theatre); Liola (National Theatre, London); The Plough and the Stars, The Passing (The Abbey); Perve (The Peacock); Theatre Club Stole Your Clock Radio, What The F&*k You Gonna Do About It? (Project/Cork); Bas Tongue, Paper Boy & Friends, Daily Bread, This is a Still Life, The Cripple of Inishmaan (Project).

Film & Television: Love/Hate, Raw, Out of Here, Homemade, Two Hearts, Agnes Brown, The General.

BAILEY HAYDEN *(Henry)*

Druid Theatre Company: Be Infants in Evil marks Bailey's debut with Druid.

Other Theatre Includes: Oklahoma, (Mount Temple School, Dublin); Ports Rock (The Complex Theatre, Dublin).

Film & Television: Tyrant (Fox21); Cop's & Robbers (Plato Films UK); Suckers Treatment (TG4/Zanzibar Films); Ceart Agus Coir (TG4/Midas Productions); Milk Run (Dejavu Productions); Exit Poll (Half a Giraffe).

Bailey has undertaken various short training courses at RADA London and The Lir Dublin.

CREATIVE TEAM

BRIAN MARTIN *(Writer)*

Be Infants in Evil is Brian's first full length play.

Brian attended the Advanced Playwriting Course taught by Marina Carr while at Trinity College, Dublin. His short play Joker Choker won Best New Writing and Best Production at the Irish Student Drama Association Festival 2009. He has also been part of the Royal Court Young Writers' Programme (2012) and Studio Group (2013).

As an actor, Brian trained at LAMDA, graduating in 2011. He most recently played the role of Chiron in the highly acclaimed production of Titus Andronicus at Shakespeare's Globe Theatre in London. Other theatre credits include: Damned by Despair, Juno and the Paycock (National Theatre, London), Stars in the Morning Sky (Belgrade Theatre, Coventry), Oliver Twist (Gate Theatre, Dublin), The Wake, Macbeth (Abbey Theatre, Dublin).

ALYSON CUMMINS *(Designer)*

Druid Theatre Company: Be Infants in Evil marks Alyson's Debut with Druid.

Set Design Includes: The Risen People, Quietly, Perve, No Escape (Abbey Theatre); The Trailer of Bridget Dinnigan (ITM); Off Plan (RAW at the Project Arts Centre).

Set & Costume Design Includes: Summertime (Tinderbox at The Mac, Belfast); It's a Family Affair - We'll Settle it Ourselves (Sherman Cymru); How to Succeed in Business Without Really Trying (The Company at the Lowry, Salford); Mixed Marriage (Lyric Theatre, Belfast); Before it Rains (Bristol Old Vic & Sherman Cymru); Pornography (Waking Exploits); Pigeon (Carpet Theatre); Ruben Guthrie (Iron Bark); How the World Began (Tom Atkins, Arcola Theatre); Hamlet (Second Age); Colleen Bawn (Project/Civic/Bedrock); Serious Money, Dying City (Rough Magic/AIB SEEDS); Extremities, Spark to a Flame; Crosswired (East London Dance Festival); The Trials of Brother Jero; Through a Film Darkly (Arambe); Ya Get Me (Old Vic education).

Associate Designer (for Rae Smith): The Prince of the Pagodas (Birmingham Royal Ballet); Rite of Spring & Petrushka (Fabulous Beast).

Alyson studied architecture at UCD and trained at Motley. She was a finalist in the Linbury biennial prize for stage design 2007.

OONAGH MURPHY *(Director)*

Druid Theatre Company: Be Infants in Evil marks Oonagh's Debut with Druid.

Oonagh's Credits Include: Associate director, The Weir at Wyndhams Theatre/Donmar West End, January 2014; assistant director, Coriolanus, National Theatre Live/Donmar Warehouse, January 2014; director The Tinkers' Wedding at The Lir, National Academy of Dramatic Art, Dublin, March 2014; assistant director Roots, The Same Deep Water as Me and The Night Alive all at the Donmar Warehouse, 2013. She directed Ribbons and Love in a Glass Jar for the Peacock Stage at the Abbey Theatre, February 2013; Taking Back Our Voices commissioned by the Abbey Theatre in collaboration with Ruhama for the Abbey Stage, November 2012; Maeve's House for the Peacock Stage, as part of the Dublin Theatre Festival In-Development strand, 2012; SQUAT at Solstice as part of Cork Midsummer Festival, 2012; Do You Read Me? presented by Talking Shop Ensemble with Shaun Dunne, at Smock Alley Theatre, as part of Absolut Fringe, 2011; I am a Home Bird (It's Very Hard) presented by Talking Shop Ensemble with Shaun Dunne, at Project Arts Centre, March 2011; Solstice as part of Cork Midsummer Festival and Electric Picnic, 2011; Anne and Barry: What Kind of Time Do You Call This? and FAT, presented by Talking Shop Ensemble as part of Absolut Fringe, 2009 and 2010 respectively; 1984 presented at the Samuel Beckett Centre's Debut Festival, 2008.

Oonagh is a Foundation Scholar in Theatre Studies of Trinity College Dublin. She was Resident Assistant Director at the Donmar Warehouse in 2013, sponsored by Jon and NoraLee Sedmak. Before that, she was Resident Assistant Director at the Abbey Theatre Dublin from May 2011 - December 2012. Oonagh has been associate/assistant to directors Josie Rourke, Conor McPherson, James Macdonald, John Crowley, Wayne Jordan, Conall Morrison and Jimmy Faye.

STEPHEN DODD *(Lighting Designer)*

Druid Theatre Company: Be Infants in Evil marks Stephen's Debut with Druid.

Lighting Designs Include: At The National Theatre, London: Riverrun (The Emergency Room/Galway International Arts Festival); at Dublin Theatre Festival: Tom and Vera (Desperate Optimists); at Dublin Fringe Festival: Lippy (Dead Centre, winner of Best Production at Irish Times Theatre Awards 2013, and Best Design and Best Production, Dublin Fringe Festival 2013); Way Back Home (Louise White, Performance Maker); In Dog Years I'm Dead (Mirari Productions); Dogs (Emma Martin Dance, winner of Best Design and Best Production, Dublin Fringe Festival 2012); Listowel Syndrome (Emma Martin Dance).

Samuel Beckett Centre, Trinity College, Dublin.

DIRECTOR'S FOREWORD

Reading an early draft of *Be Infants in Evil*, I was struck by its innate absurdity. Characters jumped into action pushing themselves towards critical junctures at an unstoppable speed. The drama was littered with images that seemed dream-like and improbable. Yet, in ensuing readings, and over various drafts, the focus sharpened, revealing a world I knew intimately. Over the past months, the key conversations between Brian, Thomas (dramaturg) and I, have been to do with naturalism, credibility, cause and effect, so that the drama positions itself on the bizarre frontier of stark reality. In this marriage of the outrageous and the banal, we are invited to ask pertinent questions about ourselves and this country we call Ireland.

'State-of-the-nation' has always been a formal category that fills me with unease. How does the inquisitive director engage with a text already heavy in answers, as 'state-of-the-nation' plays are inclined to be? That is what is tantalising about *Be Infants in Evil* – it's ability to thrash out ideas while avoiding dogmatism. Brian gives us characters so full of verve and unmanageability that the rhetoric is effortless. The big questions – of politics, class, religion, sexuality – tumble out casually, while the action is truly driven forward by those eternally more engaging elements – need, desire, hope, regret, guilt, despair.

June 2014: Our news-feeds are flooding with the story of the 800 babies formerly in the care of the Bon Secours Sisters found in a septic tank in Tuam. Constant debate on sexuality and the family unit dominates our television screens in advance of a referendum on marriage equality. European elections mark an ominous rise in far-right parties and their anti-diversity message. A year on from the death of Salvita Halappanavar, the Irish state still criminalises abortion except in the most limited circumstances.

The play in our hands happens in this climate. This is the state where we meet Noleen, Patrick, Jacinta and Henry; in a familiar place both relegated to the margins, and still somehow central to the Irish psyche. A play set in the sacristy of a Church in a country where, in 2011's census, only 18 per cent regularly attended mass even though 88 per cent still defined themselves as Catholic. This gap between what we were, and what we might go on to be – the potential for growth in a moment of crisis – is what Be Infants in Evil demands we examine.

Be Infants in Evil

by Brian Martin

Copyright © 2014 by Brian Martin

All Rights Reserved

BE INFANTS IN EVIL is fully protected under the copyright laws of the United States of America, the British Commonwealth, including Canada, and all other countries of the Copyright Union. All rights, including professional and amateur stage productions, recitation, lecturing, public reading, motion picture, radio broadcasting, television and the rights of translation into foreign languages are strictly reserved.

ISBN 978-0-573-11488-5

www.samuelfrench-london.co.uk

www.samuelfrench.com

FOR AMATEUR PRODUCTION ENQUIRIES

UNITED KINGDOM AND EUROPE
Plays@SamuelFrench-London.co.uk
020-7255-4302/01

UNITED STATES AND CANADA
Info@SamuelFrench.com
1-866-598-8449

Each title is subject to availability from Samuel French, depending upon country of performance. Please be aware that *BE INFANTS IN EVIL* may not be licensed by Samuel French in your territory. Amateur producers should contact the nearest Samuel French office or licensing partner to verify availability.

CAUTION: Professional and amateur producers are hereby warned that *BE INFANTS IN EVIL* is subject to a licensing fee. Publication of this play does not imply availability for performance. Both amateurs and professionals considering a production are strongly advised to apply to the appropriate agent before starting rehearsals, advertising, or booking a theatre. A licensing fee must be paid whether the title is presented for charity or gain and whether or not admission is charged.

The professional rights in this play are controlled by Curtis Brown, Haymarket House, 28-29 Haymarket, London SW1Y 4SP.

No one shall make any changes in this title for the purpose of production. No part of this book may be reproduced, stored in a retrieval system, or transmitted in any form, by any means, now known or yet to be invented, including mechanical, electronic, photocopying, recording, videotaping, or otherwise, without the prior written permission of the publisher. No one shall upload this title, or part of this title, to any social media websites.

AUTHOR'S ACKNOWLEDGEMENTS

Lucy Bailey, Leo Butler, Thomas Conway, Caitriona Ennis, Peter Hanly, Ciarán Hinds, Garry Hynes, Craig Flaherty, Tom Lyons, Marion Marrs, Nick Marston, Conall Morrisson, Janet Moran, James Murphy, Oonagh Murphy, Bríd Ní Neachtain, Rose Parkinson, Tom Ross-Williams, Louise Stephens Alexander, Fintan Walsh, Sarah Wolf, Camilla Young.

To everyone at Druid.

And Mom, Dad and Sarah.

For Graham,

You are the reason I want to turn over the page to find out what happens next.

"Listening to both sides of a story will convince you that there is more to a story than both sides."

FRANK TYGER

CHARACTERS

PRIEST Dublin, forty
NOLEEN Dublin, seventies
JACINTA Dublin, twenties
HENRY London, twelve

SETTING

Dublin. The sacristy of a church in Churchtown.
Present day.

NOTES ON THE TEXT

A forward slash (/) indicates an overlap in speech.

An ellipsis (…) indicates when a character is searching for a word or their thought trails off.

Dialogue in round brackets ( ) indicates a digression or afterthought.

Dialogue in square brackets [ ] is unspoken.

This text went to press before the end of rehearsals and may therefore differ slightly from the play as performed.

Dublin.

Daytime.

A Sacristy.

The colours are dull, the furniture's worn down, and the walls are scattered with Catholic iconography. The room is free from anything modern and the air is stale but the room is tidy. There is a small kitchen area and three doors: one (stage right) leads outside; another (stage left) leads to the altar of the church; and the final one (upstage) leads to a small, tiled bathroom.

A handsome priest, Irish (Dublin), forty, is dressed in black trousers and a black shirt with a white clerical collar. He is alone in the room kneeling at a prie-dieu praying in silence. We get the sense he has been praying for some time. When he finishes he blesses himself and stands. His manner is calm and his actions are measured. He looks down at the prie-dieu, opens the armrest, and peers inside the small compartment. He then realises he is not wearing his black jacket. He goes to the wardrobe and puts it on, then looks at himself in the mirror a while, making sure he looks neat. He closes the wardrobe and returns to the prie-dieu.

Unbeknownst to him an old woman, Irish (Dublin), seventies, enters through the door (stage left), stands, and looks in his direction. She is wearing black shoes, brown tights, a long dull-coloured coat, a simple silk headscarf, and luminous wayfarer-style sunglasses.

The **PRIEST**, *still looking in the compartment, now puts his hand inside and is about to pull something out when…*

NOLEEN Hello.

PRIEST Jesus!

*The **PRIEST** jumps and drops what was in his hand. He closes the armrest and leans over the prie-dieu.* **NOLEEN** *appears unaffected by any of his actions.*

NOLEEN Mary and Joseph. Great, aren't they?

*The **PRIEST** remains facing away as he tries to calm his breathing.*

NOLEEN Janey mac, what's that I'm smellin'?

NOLEEN *sniffs the air.*

PRIEST Noleen…

NOLEEN Ah how are ye, Father?

PRIEST You/ (Jesus)

NOLEEN Ye well?

PRIEST What are you doing?

NOLEEN I'm grand, thanks.

PRIEST No, *what* are you doing? Back here?

NOLEEN Well isn't that funny now, I was going to ask you the same thing.

PRIEST

NOLEEN About confession. Yer not in yer box.

PRIEST Confession?

NOLEEN Yes, now, I know I usually come/on a Friday…

PRIEST Oh, confe…it's cancelled!

NOLEEN Cancelled?

PRIEST Yes, cancelled. I put up posters.

NOLEEN Of what?

PRIEST Saying it's cancelled. Confession's cancelled, Noleen.

NOLEEN It isn't.

PRIEST It is.

NOLEEN I didn't know that.

PRIEST Well, there you go.

NOLEEN There were posters, were there?

PRIEST Everywhere.

NOLEEN And how was I supposed to see them?

> *The **PRIEST** stops, turns around to look at **NOLEEN** and realises his mistake.*

PRIEST Yes, of course, sorry, I/ …

NOLEEN Ah don't be sorry, I'm only messin' with ye. *(beat)* Anyway Father, I'm here to make me confession. I done somethin' which, I mean, at least I think…but I'd never mean to hurt anyone though, ever…*(beat)* Are you all right, Father?

PRIEST I'm fine.

NOLEEN You seem awful quiet there.

PRIEST You just caught me at a bad time.

NOLEEN Oh it's awful weather.

PRIEST Is there any chance/ we could…

NOLEEN When'll it stop?

PRIEST Do this another time…

NOLEEN God knows.

PRIEST Maybe?

NOLEEN And the amount of cars.

PRIEST Noleen.

NOLEEN Like mad.

PRIEST Noleen.

NOLEEN If they're not parked they're zoomin'.

PRIEST Listen to me.

NOLEEN I'll get knocked down one of these days, for my sins Father!

PRIEST You won't.

NOLEEN I can see it now.

PRIEST Would/ you…

NOLEEN Zoom smack!

PRIEST Noleen.

NOLEEN That'll be the end of it.

PRIEST Would ye…

NOLEEN No escapin' it.

PRIEST Stop.

NOLEEN Might as well just shoot meself in the head now and get it over with.

This suddenly brings his attention back to the room.

PRIEST That's an awful thing to say Noleen.

NOLEEN Isn't it.

PRIEST What made you say that?

NOLEEN I think I'm smellin' somethin'/ in the air…

PRIEST Don't be saying things like that again.

NOLEEN But there's/…

PRIEST All right?

Beat.

NOLEEN I'm comin' out with awful queer stuff these days. It's me nose.

PRIEST Your, what?

NOLEEN Me nose. Actin' up. Since the blindness. Have I not told you before? Smellin' everythin'.

PRIEST Right.

NOLEEN Gone real sensitive.

PRIEST Right.

NOLEEN Would that be a science thing now?

PRIEST Em, I suppose.

NOLEEN Mad into that so ye are.

PRIEST But anyway as I was saying confession's cancelled so maybe/ if you'd like to come back…

NOLEEN I was talkin' to me grandson Billy there the other day and he's into all that science stuff too you know and we're talkin' about them poor auld nuns sacrificing their lives for God and he turns to me and he says to me, "Nan, you know that anyone can be chaste these days and still have children with this new thing called 'artificial insemination' where they place sperm in the reproductive tract of the female without ever havin' the need for any sexual intercourse"? *(beat)* He's only eight. Imagine that, Father: a world full o' pregnant virgins. Mary'd be ragin'.

PRIEST Right. Anyway/…

NOLEEN What time is it by the way?

PRIEST It's *(looking at his watch)* quarter past eleven.

NOLEEN OK.

PRIEST What?

NOLEEN Nothing.

PRIEST Do you have to be somewhere?

NOLEEN I do actually. The toilet. Do you mind?

Beat.

PRIEST No, it's just around…here I'll show you.

He takes her.

PRIEST There you are now.

NOLEEN Thanks, Father.

PRIEST Mind yourself.

NOLEEN I'll be grand. It's a bit cold in here. Would you mind turning the heating up?

PRIEST Yeah.

NOLEEN Yer very good.

*The **PRIEST** closes the door behind her and takes a moment. A light sound of peeing is heard. He goes to the prie-dieu and half opens the armrest. He considers moving what's inside to another part of the sacristy, but the flushing of a toilet is soon heard. He closes the lid and turns the thermostat up before **NOLEEN** re-enters.*

NOLEEN The gun!

PRIEST What?

NOLEEN I can still smell it./ Again!

PRIEST No, Noleen.

NOLEEN I can.

PRIEST That's not/ a…

NOLEEN In the air, it's there.

PRIEST It's incense.

NOLEEN Don't think so.

PRIEST All over the place.

NOLEEN I'm sure of it this time, a gun.

PRIEST Well you're wrong.

NOLEEN I'm rarely wrong.

PRIEST Well you are this time.

NOLEEN Prove it so.

PRIEST There's been no 'shooting' around here.

NOLEEN What?

PRIEST Gun powder.

NOLEEN It's not gun powder I'm smellin'.

PRIEST Then what is it?

NOLEEN The other part.

PRIEST Which part?

NOLEEN The gun part.

Beat.

PRIEST You're telling me you're smelling the *object* of a gun?

NOLEEN Yes.

PRIEST On its own.

NOLEEN Yes.

PRIEST In this room?

NOLEEN Yes.

*The **PRIEST** can't quite believe this. He looks around the room, then up to the ceiling.*

PRIEST *(challenging)* What's the lamp made of?

NOLEEN Huh?

PRIEST On the ceiling, what's it made of?

***NOLEEN** raises her nose and sniffs.*

NOLEEN Brass.

*The **PRIEST** stares up. The lamp is not visible to the audience.*

NOLEEN Is it?

PRIEST *(confidently)* No.

Beat.

NOLEEN Are you sure?

PRIEST Positive.

NOLEEN Cos I'm gettin'/ something…

PRIEST No you're not.

NOLEEN Brassy.

PRIEST It's not.

NOLEEN Up there.

PRIEST (How can you even?)

NOLEEN Let me try again.

PRIEST I think it's best to…

NOLEEN *sniffs loudly.*

PRIEST …to leave it Noleen.

NOLEEN I coulda sworn/ it was brass.

PRIEST Leave it now.

NOLEEN Hold on.

PRIEST Please.

NOLEEN No I'm definitely…

PRIEST Noleen please.

NOLEEN It's definitely brass.

PRIEST *(suddenly, aggressively)* Would I lie to you!? Would I lie to you Noleen? It's not brass, I can see it, now just leave it, please!

Long pause.

PRIEST I'm sorry Noleen I'm/ sor…

NOLEEN It's all right.

PRIEST I shouldn't have/…

NOLEEN You're grand.

PRIEST It's just…

NOLEEN Father honestly.

PRIEST Not having a great day.

NOLEEN I know.

PRIEST I'm…

Beat.

NOLEEN Why did you cancel confession, Father?

Beat.

PRIEST Does Marina, your daughter, does she know you're here?

NOLEEN She does. No she doesn't, that was a lie. She's at a birthday party with Billy, one of his pals, and Jacinta was supposed to be keepin' an eye on me. Do ye know Jacinta, me neighbour?

PRIEST Jacinta Murphy? Keep an eye on you?

NOLEEN Yeah.

The **PRIEST** *laughs at this.*

NOLEEN What?

PRIEST Nothing.

NOLEEN Em, but, she never showed up anyway so I came here by meself, but sure don't I know the way like the back of me hand?

PRIEST Well we better call her anyway and let her know you're here and she can come pick you up.

The **PRIEST** *walks over to the phone, puts the reciever to his ear and prepares to dial.*

PRIEST Do you have her number there?

NOLEEN I don't.

He hangs up the reciever, unimpressed. He walks to his desk and retrieves a very large leather-bound book – the baptismal register.

NOLEEN D'ye not like it here, Father?

PRIEST I do.

NOLEEN We don't appreciate ye, do we?

PRIEST Who?

NOLEEN Everyone. The parish.

PRIEST Of course you do.

NOLEEN As much as London?

*The **PRIEST** begins flicking through the register in search of* **'MURPHY, JACINTA'**.

NOLEEN Yer sermons are awful quick these days, Father.

PRIEST I don't do sermons any more.

NOLEEN Ah ye do, But I missed the last one ye did, the last proper one, before ye stopped. About yer man and his bang.

PRIEST Sorry?

NOLEEN Ye know, the bang. *(beat)* Em, the big one?

PRIEST (Oh, the big bang).

NOLEEN That's the one. And, now, I wasn't there (I went to the later mass) but Josephine came to mine for tea afterwards to tell me about it. Said you were ravin' about it so ye were. And then that was the end o' them. Why?

*The **PRIEST** finds the number.*

PRIEST Here we are.

He dials it into the phone.

NOLEEN She said it was somethin' to do with the…? With the…? With the…? With the…? With the…? With the/…?

PRIEST With the creation.

NOLEEN With the creation.

PRIEST Yeah.

NOLEEN And Adam and Eve.

PRIEST Yeah.

NOLEEN And she got a bit confused, she'd got lost in the middle (so maybe you can explain this to me now) but the bit about the Adams?

PRIEST The Adams?

NOLEEN That's what she said. And I had thought there was only the one as far as I could remember so there's us goin' "what's he on about now with all them Adams and just the one Eve and them all sittin' around Eden havin' a big bang?"

Beat.

PRIEST What?

NOLEEN Josephine didn't know what to think of it. Couldn't make head nor tail of it, went a bit frail, had to have coffee instead.

*The **PRIEST** hangs up the phone, agitated.*

PRIEST That's not what I said.

NOLEEN She said the silence in the church afterwards was deafenin'.

PRIEST Yes. It was.

NOLEEN And then that was the end of yer sermons.

PRIEST I doubt anyone's missing them.

NOLEEN Yes, they are.

PRIEST No, they're not.

NOLEEN Well, I am.

Beat.

PRIEST I was saying 'atoms'.

NOLEEN Adams.

PRIEST No, atoms, with a 't', aToms.

NOLEEN What's that?

PRIEST You wouldn't have her mobile number? Hold on, *you* have a mobile; your daughter just bought you one.

NOLEEN Em…

PRIEST To call her from prayer meetings or something?

NOLEEN That's right.

PRIEST Jacinta's number would be on that.

NOLEEN Em…

PRIEST Surely…

NOLEEN ...Yes.

He rolls his eyes at this.

PRIEST Where is it?

NOLEEN Em, in me bag I think.

PRIEST Here.

*He grabs **NOLEEN**'s bag trying to restrain his frustration. **NOLEEN** remains quiet as he searches through it. He pulls out three tins of cat food.*

PRIEST There's three tins of cat food in here, Noleen.

NOLEEN Oh, sorry about that.

He places them down and continues looking through the bag.

NOLEEN I don't know how they got in there. I don't even have a cat.

*The **PRIEST** eventually finds the phone. He tries to operate it but is unable.*

PRIEST How do I use this? Where's her number?

NOLEEN Em, for Jacinta ye hold down the middle button, the five it should be.

PRIEST Actually, you call her. Here.

NOLEEN Me?

PRIEST *(placing it in her hand)* Yeah, go on.

NOLEEN Why?

PRIEST Just, I don't...please.

Beat.

NOLEEN All right.

NOLEEN *carefully feels the buttons on the phone, presses the middle one, and gently holds it to her ear. After a moment's ringing:*

NOLEEN Hello? Hello Jacinta?... Yeah hello Jacinta, it's Noleen. How are ye?... I'm at the church... I am... with himself here...no just the two of us...oh ye are?...

oh right well, I'll see you soon so…thanks Jacinta, thanks…right. God bless, God bless.

She hangs up.

NOLEEN She's on her way.

NOLEEN *holds out the phone. The* **PRIEST** *takes it and puts it in her bag.*

Silence.

NOLEEN Do you not like me Father?

PRIEST What?

NOLEEN Do you not like me?

PRIEST Of course I like you Noleen, why would you say that?

NOLEEN Like, I'm feelin' a bit sad right now.

PRIEST Wh…why, are you sad?

NOLEEN Like, I'm gettin' the impression ye don't want me here or something.

PRIEST No, I do, I do want you here Noleen, it's just, it's just not the best time but I do love having you here, I do, please don't be sad.

NOLEEN That's just how I was feelin' there.

PRIEST I'm sorry if I made you feel that way, I really didn't mean it, please forgive me.

Beat.

PRIEST Would you like to say your confession?

NOLEEN Me confession?

PRIEST Yeah.

NOLEEN I thought it was cancelled?

PRIEST I've uncancelled it.

NOLEEN Ye haven't.

PRIEST I have.

NOLEEN God thanks Father, yer very kind, thank you. Right. Where am I? That's right. *(beat)* I got a phone call one day from Marina, me daughter, tellin' me there'd been an accident with Da and I'd to get ready straight away cos she was picking me up to go to the hospital. Heart attack. Behind the wheel. Luck would have it the road was empty at the time. Straight into a wall. In the car with Marina me heart was racin'. Me husband, who I'd spent all me life with, was lyin' in some Emergency Room holdin' on for dear life, waitin' for me, while I was stuck behind a red light. He was the man of me dreams, Father. *(desperately)* 'Dougie', I thought, 'I've a question for you Dougie I've been meanin' to ask you me whole life if I could just be there beside you now I need the answer please!' *(beat)* His hands were cold. He was only seventy-six, had just given up the substitute teachin' in St. Mary's National down the road and we were planning a trip, somewhere abroad ye know, somewhere foreign. He'd gone down to the shops to get milk. *(beat)* Just before he died, apparently, he was mutterin' somethin': "Brother Kelly. Brother Kelly." *(beat)* Few months after Dougie passed the girls from bridge were goin' to Medjugorje and wanted me/ to go with them...

A young woman, Irish (Dublin), twenties, suddenly rushes in through the door (stage right). She is wearing a niqab which completely covers her body except for her eyes. She is quite wet and carries a small, scrunched-up, white paper chemist bag.

JACINTA Jesus, Mary and Joseph it's bucketin' out there! I mean, it's gorgeous all day and then suddenly a freak downpour!

PRIEST Excuse me?

JACINTA I think I'm actually havin' the worst day of me life.

PRIEST Excuse me!?

JACINTA Don't you even try and 'excuse me' me, you. You have no idea what I have been through today: I wake up at the crack of dawn, really not feeling the Mae West, only for Mark to come in and start jumpin' on me bed, shoutin' "Ma! Ma! There's no Frosties left. Ma! Ma! I'm starvin'" And I keep beggin' him to "please, Mark please just leave me alone for five minutes", but of course he's havin' none of it, never does, so I says "All right! Off we go, down to Tescos, get in the car and hurry up." Get to Tescos and what happens next? I'm stopped at the entrance by some Asian eejit, rudest person I ever met in me life *(in a bad asian accent)* "Sorry mam" he says "but yer gonna have to take yer headscarf off before comin' into the shops", "Eh, 'headscarf'?" I says, "Are ya thick or wha'? It's a bleedin' niqab!" "Well you're gonna have to take it off either way mam." Meanwhile Mark is still hangin' outta me "Ma! Ma! I want Frosties, I'm starvin'!" "Would ye ever shut up!?" I says to him "I'm tryin' to get your bleedin' Frosties, if it weren't for this fuckin' racist!!!" And before I know it they're 'escortin' me away from the shops, everyone's starin', probably think I've got a bomb strapped to me or somethin', and I've had it up to here by now, so d'ye know wha I do? I pull out me clicky pen, hold it up in the air, and start screamin' "I'll blow it up now! I'll blow it up now!" at the top of me voice "I swear to Allah, I'll blow it up if yis don't let go of me!" So they do, faster than the speed of light and everyone who's watchin' starts screamin' and whalin', runnin' away, hidin' behind cars, coverin' their kids, security are on their walkie talkies… I start hearin' police sirens in the distance, think that's our cue to leave, file into the car and legged it outta there. Thankfully no one followed us, would have been mortified otherwise. *(beat)* I am at me wit's end, I'm tellin' ye, between the kid and the racist. Anyway, get home and there was Frosties in the cupboard all along. *(To the* **PRIEST***)* Come here, there's something I need to talk to ye about. It's urgent.

NOLEEN How are ya, Jacinta?

JACINTA Oh. And then to add to all tha' this one here goes missin'.

NOLEEN I was only here.

JACINTA I was worried sick.

NOLEEN Ye weren't?

JACINTA I was.

NOLEEN Sacred heart.

JACINTA I coulda died.

NOLEEN I'm sorry Jacinta.

JACINTA Yer very selfish sometimes d'ye know tha'?

NOLEEN I do.

JACINTA No concern for how I was feelin'.

NOLEEN I left a note.

JACINTA I couldn't work it out.

NOLEEN Could ye not?

JACINTA It was all scribbles.

NOLEEN Was it?

JACINTA On the table as well, ye missed the paper.

NOLEEN Sufferin' duck.

JACINTA With permanent marker.

NOLEEN Will it come out?

JACINTA Didn't bother tryin', doesn't make a difference to you does it?

NOLEEN I suppose not.

JACINTA Can't see it either way.

NOLEEN I know.

JACINTA Anyway you're to wait for me in future.

NOLEEN I will.

JACINTA But I figured you were either in Josephine's or here.

NOLEEN Did you go to Josephine's?

JACINTA I did.

NOLEEN How was she?

JACINTA I dunno how you put up with her.

NOLEEN Why?

JACINTA Well I called to the door, and I was askin' her if you were there, when she suddenly disappeared into the back.

NOLEEN To come and get me?

Beat.

JACINTA But you weren't there though Noleen.

NOLEEN Oh right.

JACINTA You were here.

NOLEEN Oh right.

Beat.

JACINTA Anyway, I dunno what she was at, musta thought it was Halloween or somethin', next minute she comes out and starts puttin' sweets in me bag.

NOLEEN She's great for the trick-or-treatin' so she is.

JACINTA It's the middle of May, Noleen.

NOLEEN Is it not Halloween?

Beat.

JACINTA No, Noleen.

NOLEEN Oh, right.

JACINTA Halloween's in October.

NOLEEN Oh right.

Beat.

JACINTA I dunno who's worse, you or Josephine.

PRIEST But everything's all right now.

JACINTA What do you think, Nolers?

NOLEEN Yes.

PRIEST She's been safe, in case you're interested.

JACINTA Thank God for tha'.

NOLEEN Thank God.

Beat.

JACINTA What d'ye think of her new shades, Father? Got them for her on me holidays.

PRIEST

JACINTA They'll keep the sun out, won't they, Nolers?

NOLEEN They will.

Beat.

JACINTA Speakin' of which, it's abnormally roastin' in here.

PRIEST Noleen was feeling the cold.

NOLEEN I feel the cold.

JACINTA I'm sweatin' buckets now, can I take it off?

The **PRIEST**, *losing his patience, gestures for her to do so.*

JACINTA Could do with dryin' it as well.

NOLEEN Have you still got yer coat on?

JACINTA Eh. Yeah Noleen. Me coat.

NOLEEN Well take it off so.

JACINTA I will. Thanks.

JACINTA places the chemist bag on the counter. As she begins to take off her niqab a mobile phone rings: the 'Ghostbusters' theme tune. It plays as if in sync with her impending identity revelation. The music builds as she slowly pulls the niqab up over her head and, just as she takes everything off to reveal her face, the beat kicks in. She is looking quite flashy. The phone rings to no response for a while. They all stand there, unsure of what's happening.

NOLEEN *(suddenly)* Oh that's me ringtone! Where's me bag?

NOLEEN begins sniffing the air to see if she can locate her bag. Meanwhile the PRIEST retrieves it and hands it to her while JACINTA hangs up her niqab in the bathroom.

PRIEST Here.

NOLEEN Yer very good. *(she takes the phone and walks towards the stage right door)* Hello? Hello?… Ah how are ya?… Good thanks. Ye found yer way to the LUAS all right?… Ah good, good, not long now…

NOLEEN *exits.* **JACINTA** *and the* **PRIEST** *are left in silence. A tension simmers.*

JACINTA Yeah. So. I wanted to speak to you in/ private anyway so…

PRIEST What's with the burka?

JACINTA It's a niqab. Ignorant.

Beat.

JACINTA Anyways, I wanted to/ speak to ye…

PRIEST I just had an elderly blind woman walk all the way from her house here to the church by *herself* when *you* were supposed to be keeping an eye on her.

JACINTA That wasn't my fault.

PRIEST Whose fault was it then?

JACINTA She shouldn't have left.

PRIEST No, *you* shouldn't have left her alone.

JACINTA I had other things to be doing.

PRIEST Like what? Abandoning your own child on his communion day again?

Beat.

JACINTA Excuse me?

PRIEST Where were you?

JACINTA That is none of yer business.

PRIEST Jacinta, I had to hold his hand, on the altar, in front of the entire church, for the entire ceremony.

JACINTA I'm not discussin' this with you.

PRIEST One of the mothers organised a special collection just for Mark, to stop him crying.

JACINTA If you knew an ounce of what I'd been through.

PRIEST Where were you?

JACINTA That's not why I'm here.

PRIEST Then why are you here?

Beat.

JACINTA I've good news for ye. None of that's ever gonna happen again. Things are different now. Cos I've met someone.

NOLEEN *re-enters as* **JACINTA** *says this.*

NOLEEN You've met someone?

JACINTA That's right, Nolers.

NOLEEN Ye didn't.

JACINTA I did.

NOLEEN Ah go 'way, what's his name?

JACINTA Gafar.

NOLEEN Gafar? That's very tropical.

JACINTA Yeah, but do ye know Aladdin?

NOLEEN (Do I know Aladdin?) It's only me favourite film.

JACINTA Well it's like yer man Jafar but with a 'G'.

NOLEEN Really? Is he evil so?

JACINTA No, he's not evil Noleen.

NOLEEN What's he like then?

JACINTA Where to start? He is the most romantic person I ever met in me life.

NOLEEN God.

JACINTA Like, I'm in love Noleen, literally, I can't even describe the feelin's to ye.

NOLEEN Wow.

JACINTA And get this right, I mean, you are not even gonna believe this part now.

NOLEEN Which part now?

JACINTA He's an oil baron.

NOLEEN He is not.

JACINTA Minted, so he is. But like, not what ye'd think now. He is the kindest gentleman ye ever met in yer life. He treats me, like, I've never even known.

NOLEEN How'd ye meet him?

JACINTA I was in Dubai there, sure ye know, on me holidays.

NOLEEN I know but ye've told me nothin' about it, why or how.

JACINTA Ah right, well I went with me mate Kirsty, right, who was supposed to be goin' there on her honeymoon with her husband Ger, they'd just got married like, only she caught him sleepin' with her Ma, like, on their weddin' night so she asked me to go instead, I was delighted. (I think they went on a break or something but they're back together now so it's all right. Her Ma's up the duff with yer man now but they're gonna keep it and just give it to Kirsty anyway cos she's barren.) So anyways, she asked me if I'd go instead. All I'd to pay for was me flights and I couldn't afford it initially but then me circumstances changed so away we went/ …

PRIEST Why don't you tell Noleen *how* your circumstances changed?

JACINTA is silenced, staring at the PRIEST. Eventually she turns to NOLEEN and carries on.

JACINTA So we were on the beach right. Noleen? And I went in for a little swim, and I knew I shouldn'ta had all them chips for lunch but I start gettin' a stitch and next minute I'm drownin', goin' under, start screamin' for help. Suddenly, I feel this arm come around me head, some fella starts bringin' me back into the shore, and as it gets shallow enough to stand I turn around and see him: gorgeous! He walks me back to the sand and says, "I take you out of the water, now I take you out to dinner".

NOLEEN Ah would ye listen.

JACINTA And guess where he takes me? Only up the top of the bleedin' Burj Khalifa.

NOLEEN The where?

JACINTA It's like the tallest tower in the world Nolers, mad expensive. But sure I'd no idea where we'd be goin', he only told me to meet him at this market nearby, I didn't know/ nothin'.

PRIEST OK! And?

JACINTA And wha'?

PRIEST What has that got to do with anything?

Beat.

JACINTA He's asked me to marry him.

NOLEEN He hasn't.

JACINTA He has.

NOLEEN Ah, Jacinta!

JACINTA I know.

NOLEEN Isn't that great.

JACINTA Thanks Noleen.

NOLEEN I'm delighted for ye.

JACINTA And you, Father?

NOLEEN Wait til Marina hears.

PRIEST What?

JACINTA Aren't ye happy for me?

Beat.

PRIEST No. I think it's stupid.

JACINTA Excuse me?

PRIEST You've only just met him, what, this week?

JACINTA Four weeks ago. And I love him.

PRIEST Really? You love him?

JACINTA Eh, yeah, actually, I do.

PRIEST Don't be so naïve, Jacinta!

JACINTA And what do *you* know exactly about love, huh?

PRIEST Enough to know/ when it's…

JACINTA Nothin'! Do ye? Yer a priest. Ye gave it all up, what's it called? Chastity isn't it? Ye stand up there on the altar every day preaching wha', 'love', is to all five members left of the church, when you yourself don't even have the faintest idea what yer talkin' about, do ye?

PRIEST Jacinta/ …

JACINTA Do ye?! *(beat)* Anyway, I don't need to put up with yer commentin' anymore, and you won't have to put up with me. I'm defectin'.

NOLEEN Defectin'?

JACINTA Noleen.

NOLEEN What's that mean?

JACINTA Never mind.

NOLEEN I'm only askin'.

JACINTA Leave out of it.

NOLEEN What's she doin' Father?

JACINTA It's none o' yer business.

NOLEEN Defectin'?

JACINTA Yeah, from the church.

NOLEEN What's tha' mean?

JACINTA Can ye not just stay out of it?

NOLEEN Defectin'?

JACINTA Yes, I'm defectin' Noleen! I'm feckin' off, defectin'.

NOLEEN Defectin'?

JACINTA Yes defectin'. How many more times do I have to say it? Defectin'!

Beat.

NOLEEN Oh, defectin'?

JACINTA Yes, defectin'.

NOLEEN Oh, right.

Beat.

NOLEEN What's tha' mean?

JACINTA (Lord, give me patience) I'm leavin' the church/…

NOLEEN Why?

JACINTA Have ye told Marina the good news yet?

NOLEEN What?

JACINTA That I'm getting married.

NOLEEN No,/ but…

JACINTA Well call her there now and tell her, she'll be delighted to hear. And it's sunny again, why don't we go outside?

NOLEEN Is it sunny again, is it?

JACINTA Splittin' the trees.

NOLEEN I do like the sun on me face.

JACINTA *(helping Noleen to the stage right door)* You do an' all. Perfect. Come on so.

NOLEEN Yer very good to me, Jacinta.

JACINTA I know I am, Nolers.

NOLEEN I'm fine from here.

JACINTA Ye sure?

NOLEEN Honestly, there's a bench just there.

> **NOLEEN** *exits and* **JACINTA** *returns to the Sacristy. The* **PRIEST** *looks at her, amused and confused.*

PRIEST You're defecting?

JACINTA Yeah.

PRIEST Why?

JACINTA What ye mean 'why'?

PRIEST Why do you need *official* proof you're leaving the church? You're hardly a practicing Catholic, Jacinta and if I'm being honest this all seems a bit suspect.

JACINTA Because his Da's a sheikh. All right? Beautiful human being, so wise, and generous, I love him to bits. But he takes all this very seriously. We had this big sit-down meetin' and…he wants the archbishop to speak with him directly, after I've 'formally defected', *otherwise*…All right? (**JACINTA** *searches through her bag for the sheikh's number*) So that's what I need you to do now, is call the archbishop there and let him know I'm out. Please. And I'm flying out to Dubai tomorrow so if you wouldn't mind I'm kinda in a rush.

PRIEST *Tomorrow?*

JACINTA That's what I said.

PRIEST

JACINTA What?

PRIEST What does your son think of him?

Beat.

JACINTA Why?

PRIEST Well if he's going to be his father?

JACINTA He's not his father though, is he?

PRIEST Yet, surely?

JACINTA

PRIEST You haven't told him about Mark, have you? Have you?

JACINTA I went to the pub *(beat)* You want to know where I went on Mark's communion, I went to the pub. I dropped him off, said I was parkin' the car, and I went to the pub. I drank the place dry, got back in the car, music blarin', and I drove. Down the road, onto the M50, and I drove. I fuckin' drove. I drove, and I drove, and I drove faster, and faster, and faster again, the car revvin' so fuckin' loud I could hardly hear myself screamin', shoutin' to God, praying for it to just all be over until the worst thing that could have possibly happened *happened*. And d'ye know what that was? Nothin'. Nothin' at all. I got home. Pulled into the drive. And I cried. I cried and I cried until I couldn't cry anymore. Fell asleep in the car. Later me Ma came round. She picked up Mark but missed the communion *(laughing)* I couldn't even tell her the right time! She was not happy, woke me up. "What the hell are ye at?" she said. So I told her. Then she told me about the communion money. Mark's 'special collection'. I didn't believe her when she said how much, but then she showed it me. I couldn't believe it! That mornin' Kirsty'd asked me to go to Dubai and I couldn't afford it cos of Mark. He almost killed me but now this was goin' to save me. So I took it. Rightfully. And off I went. *(beat)* I'm goin' back to

Dubai tomorrow. Me Ma's takin' Mark. Cos she loves her child. I don't. And that's tha'.

Beat.

PRIEST So first you abandon your child on his communion day, and now you're going to abandon him entirely?

JACINTA I think it'd be best if you call up yer friend, the archbishop there, and tell him Jacinta Murphy would like her name removed from the Catholic register straight away, and to call Sheikh Rashid bin Hushur in Dubai asap to confirm it, I've a number for ye here *(she hands him the piece of paper from her bag)* and that it's in *both* yer interests to do so as quickly as possible, because the archbishop was the man who so nicely removed you from your London parish and *secretly* relocated you here without any questions asked. Am I right?

The temperature changes.

PRIEST You should be careful with the choice of words you use Jacinta,/ what you're suggesting is…

JACINTA Is that a threat?

PRIEST No, what you're suggesting is/ …

JACINTA Is what?

*Beat. The **PRIEST** goes to the phone. He searches for his address book to retrieve the archbishop's number and dials. **JACINTA** goes to the bathroom to put her niqab back on, but just before she does…*

JACINTA Father.

PRIEST What?

JACINTA Thanks.

***JACINTA** continues to re-dress herself. The **PRIEST** turns back to the phone. Suddenly, the little white paper bag on the counter grabs the **PRIEST**'s attention. He turns round to see **JACINTA** is not looking, then back to the bag. Curiosity gets the better of him. Slowly, he picks it up and peers inside. A look of concern crosses his face.*

PRIEST Jacinta…

JACINTA Gimme a sec.

*The **PRIEST** slowly puts the phone back on the receiver.*
***JACINTA** finally manages to put her niqab on correctly.*

JACINTA What?

***JACINTA** sees what the **PRIEST** is looking at and snatches the bag out of his hand.*

JACINTA What d'ye think yer doin'?

PRIEST What is that?

JACINTA It's nothin'.

PRIEST Doesn't look like nothing.

JACINTA Well, that's what it is.

PRIEST It looked like a pregnancy test.

JACINTA Well it's not a pregnancy test/ all right?

PRIEST A *used* pregnancy test.

JACINTA What are you doin' rootin'/ through me…?

PRIEST Are you pregnant, Jacinta?

JACINTA It's private!

Beat.

PRIEST I'm not making any phone call unless you tell me what's going on here.

Beat.

JACINTA I don't know yet.

PRIEST What?

JACINTA If I'm pregnant.

PRIEST Why not?

JACINTA Cos it's broken, it didn't work.

PRIEST The test.

JACINTA Yeah, it didn't work, I used it and it didn't say annythin' either way, it said nothin' cos it didn't work so I'm going back to the chemist now to get a new one but it's closing early today, so if you wouldn't mind hurryin' up makin' that phone call I'm kinda in a rush.

PRIEST Go tomorrow.

JACINTA I'm flyin' tomorrow.

Beat.

PRIEST Have you told Gafar yet?

JACINTA What about?

PRIEST His child.

JACINTA No.

PRIEST Why not?

JACINTA It's not his!

JACINTA *immediately regrets revealing this information.*

PRIEST Excuse me? Then what if it's positive?

JACINTA None of yer business.

PRIEST Jesus Christ.

JACINTA It's my decision.

PRIEST What? Hold on. OK. No. I'm not stupid Jacinta. If that test is positive…no, I won't have it.

JACINTA Have what? It's nothing to do with you.

PRIEST Oh is it not? Then call the archbishop yourself. Go on. Renounce your Catholicism directly. And while you're at it have him tell the 'Oil Barons of Dubai' that you're pregnant with *someone else's* child, but not to worry because you're planning on getting rid of it anyway. Or would you rather I called him? Oh no wait. You *need* me to. But I never will. Because the archbishop will never speak to this Sheikh of yours and there'll never be any point in killing the innocent when you've no fairytale romance to fly away to, will there? So with that in mind I think we can safely say we're done here.

Beat.

JACINTA No. You're not stupid. Are ye?

PRIEST No.

JACINTA No. Me neither. *(beat)* Who's Mrs E. Carter?

The **PRIEST** *is still.*

JACINTA Ye know Mumsnet? That site in England where mas talk all sorts of middle class shite about their kids: the best schools, the best dinners, the best *tutors* – cos that's what they call it in England, don't they? 'Tutorin'' isn't it? Not grinds. Well ye must know it, cos yer name popped up on it. And some ma called Mrs E. Carter on some old forum was talking about 'recommendin'' tutors to use for yer kids' and she just couldn't speak any higher of you. The incredible things she was sayin' about how you miraculously turned her son Henry's life around; *Henry's* now this and *Henry's* now that. So I think to meself "best get on to this woman, see if he's the same forward-thinkin' priest come to our parish, cos he could sort me out with me defection and the archbishop an' all". So I email her. About you. And d'ye know what she replied?

Long pause.

PRIEST Jacinta/ I…

JACINTA Sure the test could be negative still and all this an unnecessary hoo-ha. Anyway *(checking her watch)* I don't have time to be dilly-dallyin' about here any longer. I'm gonna leg it down to the chemist there and sort this out. And while I'm gone I expect that phone call to be gettin' made (**JACINTA** *walks towards the door, turns)* Otherwise, I suspect you'll be movin' parish again. Won't ye?

She exits. The **PRIEST** *is left on his own for a while.*
NOLEEN *re-enters.*

NOLEEN Sometimes I like to pretend I'm an alien. Ye know what I mean Father? Like I'm not from here and I don't understand anythin' and I'm just observin' everythin' and not involved at all, and when ye think about it, all we really are is just livin' things on this revolving thing doing things to other things…and whoever got to decide whether these things were 'good' or 'bad' at all? Ye know? Whatever 'good' and 'bad' mean at all in the first place cos they mean different things all the time, don't they Father? *(beat)* Is there something different about Jacinta now, Father or is it just me?

PRIEST Weren't you meant to be going with her, Noleen?

NOLEEN Oh, but, I didn't finish me confession Father. Will I finish it now?

PRIEST

NOLEEN Few months after Dougie passed the girls from bridge were goin' to Medjugorje on pilgrimage and wanted me to go with them, thought it would be good for me. And Marina insisted on payin'. I wasn't in the mood but there was no point in arguin', I was goin'. Beautiful place. Anyway, off I went by meself one day, found a quiet spot, had a sit. Now, I'd heard stories of things happenin' there, mysteries and all that, and before I know it I find meself starin' up at the sun, captivated, and gradually it's startin' to move, spin like, it's dancin' around the sky like a tennis ball bouncin' up and down when suddenly I feel a massive jolt in me head pullin' me backwards and everythin's turnin' white *(slow)* It's quiet, and then, in the centre of it all, out emerges, slowly, the Virgin Mary herself. *(pause)* She's the most beautiful thing I've ever seen in me entire life, comin towards me, I'm feelin' warm and fuzzy all over can't stop smilin'. "Mary", I says to her, "Mary? You wouldn't happen to know me husband, Dougie?" She's noddin', gently like. "I, I don't want to sound rude or nothin' Mary, but is there any chance I could speak to him one more time please? There's somethin' I need to ask him." "Of course", she says as she's smiling, "but, you must give me something in return." "Anythin'" I says "I'll give you anythin' Mary." "Good," she says. "What is it?" I ask. "Your eyesight Noleen. In order to see the truth you must be blinded to all that is false around you, for all who follow that shall surely burn in the eternal fires of hell." *(beat)*

Dougie was the last thing I remember seein', standin' there, in the light, alone. I asked him me question. He remained silent for a long time, starin' at me, blankly. Eventually his lips began to move. "Yes," he said. "*Yes*". *(becoming very emotional and bringing her head to her hands)* I've never been the same since.

Pause.

PRIEST What did you ask him?

Slowly, **NOLEEN** *raises her head. But, just as she goes to speak, the church bells begin to ring.*

NOLEEN I'd better go.

NOLEEN *suddenly turns and starts heading back into the church.*

PRIEST Where?

NOLEEN In here.

PRIEST Why?

NOLEEN The angelus.

PRIEST The…? What? Noleen?

NOLEEN Yes?

PRIEST What was the question?

Beat.

NOLEEN I won't be long Father. Jacinta'll be back soon.

She exits. The **PRIEST** *is still. But not for long. He turns to look at the prie-dieu and stares at the armrest. But, as the bell tolls for the twelfth time, a twelve year-old boy, English (RP), enters (stage right) and stands in the doorway.*

HENRY. Hello, Patrick

The **PRIEST** *(now* **PATRICK***) turns around.*

Long pause.

HENRY I don't bite my nails anymore.

PATRICK …What?

HENRY I don't bite my nails anymore.

PATRICK Oh. That's…great.

HENRY Yeah.

PATRICK Why?

HENRY Why what?

PATRICK Did you stop?

HENRY Oh, just, because…you know?

PATRICK Yeah.

HENRY Yeah. I've also been getting really into the History Channel lately, I know I always said it was boring and didn't even compare/ to the Discovery Channel.

PATRICK Henry what are you doing here?

HENRY What am I…? I'm visiting, *we're* visiting.

PATRICK Who's 'we'?

HENRY Mum and I.

PATRICK Your mum's here?

HENRY Yeah.

PATRICK Where?

HENRY She dropped me off.

PATRICK Here?

HENRY Yeah.

PATRICK She knows you're here?

HENRY Yes.

Beat.

PATRICK Where is she now?

HENRY She's visiting people.

PATRICK Who?

HENRY I dunno, people.

PATRICK Henry.

HENRY She is, she's got friends or something from University she hasn't seen in ages so she dropped me off here and she's gone off to see them and she's coming by later.

PATRICK …I don't believe you.

HENRY What?

PATRICK I don't believe you.

HENRY …OK.

> **PATRICK** *is on-edge.*

HENRY Oh and she had a letter she wanted me to give to you.

> **HENRY** *opens his bag and retrieves a sealed envelope. He holds it out to* **PATRICK.**

HENRY She said she wanted to apologise for something, or something.

> *Hesitantly,* **PATRICK** *takes the letter, opens it and reads it. This calms his tension somewhat.*

PATRICK I haven't spoken to her.

HENRY I know. But she says that's ok, it happens to people sometimes, they move on and fall out of touch. She's really looking forward to seeing you though.

PATRICK

HENRY Do you have coffee by any chance? I've really got into coffee lately.

PATRICK Eh, yeah. On the counter there.

HENRY Where? Oh, *instant?!* Surely not instant, Patrick. Come now, you must have at least ground.

PATRICK *(amused)* I do, in the cupboard.

HENRY Which? This one?

PATRICK No.

> **HENRY** *indicates another cupboard.*

PATRICK Yeah.

HENRY Ah yes. Strength 4, brilliant, and the cafetiere?

PATRICK Should be there.

HENRY *(finds)* Cool beans.

> **HENRY** *pours some water into the kettle, stops.*

HENRY Want some?

PATRICK Please.

> **HENRY** *pours more in, stops.*

HENRY Mum is always telling me to only boil the amount of water I need so as to save the environment.

He boils the kettle.

PATRICK That's right.

HENRY But I keep telling her "Mum, it only takes about 300 kilojoules to boil the kettle in the first place, you're hardly going to stop the world from being destroyed by boiling only one cup of water", but then she's like "every little helps, Henry" and I'm like "Mum stop quoting Tescos" and that shuts her up cos she only likes shopping at Waitrose.

PATRICK *smiles.*

HENRY You used to drink it all the time at my house.

PATRICK I know. Well I needed it to keep up with you.

HENRY I always loved the smell of it.

PATRICK Mm.

HENRY But the taste was bloody awful.

PATRICK I remember you trying it actually.

HENRY Oh God.

PATRICK You took one sip and sprayed it everywhere.

HENRY *(laughing)* Yeah.

PATRICK And then you gave it back to me as if I still wanted it.

HENRY It was a perfectly good cup!

PATRICK That had been backwashed and spat back in? No thanks! That was good coffee your mum used to get actually. Organic of course.

HENRY Of course.

Beat.

HENRY I've taken up cycling too.

PATRICK Oh yeah?

HENRY Yeah, got a racer and everything, cycle everywhere.

PATRICK Very cool.

HENRY Do you still?

PATRICK No, not so much.

HENRY Since when?

PATRICK Since here.

HENRY Why?

PATRICK Just, no need. I have everything on my doorstep.

HENRY But what about cycling aimlessly? Wherever you want? Being a *flâneur de cyclisme*?

PATRICK Oh my God you remembered that?

HENRY Of course.

PATRICK Jaysus. What am I like?

HENRY I know, a bit naff, but hey.

PATRICK Excuse me? I'll be the one to decide what's naff and what's not, OK?

HENRY Oh really?

PATRICK Yes really, Mr '300-kilojoules-to-boil-the-kettle'.

HENRY How's that naff?

PATRICK It's very pernickety.

HENRY But it's not naff.

PATRICK Being pernickety is pretty naff these days.

HENRY I was only being specific.

PATRICK Sure you weren't trying to show off?

HENRY I thought you liked specificity.

PATRICK I do.

HENRY Well what's wrong with knowing how many kilojoules my kettle takes to boil?

PATRICK *(holding back laughter)* Nothing.

HENRY Why are you laughing?

PATRICK I'm not, I'm sorry.

Beat.

HENRY *(inhales)* You're jealous!

PATRICK What?

HENRY You're so jealous!

PATRICK Why?

HENRY Because *I* knew something you didn't.

PATRICK Eh, I don't think so.

HENRY Oh I do, I saw it in your eye when I said it, you felt threatened.

PATRICK By useless information?

HENRY Which is your strong point, *was* your strong point.

PATRICK Still *is* my strong point.

HENRY Not anymore. Henry Carter takes first place.

PATRICK I don't think so.

HENRY *(enjoying this)* Look at you, you're so jealous!

PATRICK Oh yeah?

HENRY Yes.

PATRICK Then how many kilojoules does it take to run, say, a fridge each day?

Beat.

HENRY That's not fair.

PATRICK Oh do you not know the answer?

HENRY No.

PATRICK I thought you knew your kilojoules though?

HENRY Not for everything.

PATRICK Not very specific so.

HENRY That's a stupid question.

PATRICK Ah well, second place is still good.

HENRY What's the most popular name in the world then?

PATRICK Where did that come from?

HENRY Oh do you not know the answer?

PATRICK That question had nothing to do with the last one.

HENRY Oh well, second place is still good.

PATRICK Getting a bit competitive now are we?

HENRY No, I'm just better.

PATRICK Oh really?

HENRY Yeah.

Pause.

PATRICK 'Mohammed', supposedly, and come on, that was easy. See, you got me wrong Henry: 'useless information' isn't my strong point, 'information' is my strong point, some of which just happens to be useless.

Checkmate.

PATRICK Coffee?

HENRY *(playfully)* Ugh, you're such a dick.

PATRICK Oh my word, can we keep the language civil please?

HENRY The smirk on your face.

PATRICK *(relishing the glory)* Milk? Sugar?

HENRY You love it, look at you.

PATRICK *(innocently defensive)* I just love making coffee.

HENRY Do you even know what it feels like to be wrong?

PATRICK I don't know, you tell me.

HENRY Oh you're *such* a/…

PATRICK 'Genius' I do believe is the correct term.

HENRY ('Dick' more like).

PATRICK What was that?

HENRY *Milk*! I said, please.

PATRICK Oh 'milk' was it?

HENRY Yep.

PATRICK And sugar?

HENRY No.

PATRICK To sweeten the bitterness maybe?

HENRY I quite like bitterness actually.

PATRICK Doesn't suit you though.

HENRY Makes me look menacing.

PATRICK You look better when you smile.

A moment. The coffee is distributed.

PATRICK How's school going?

HENRY Fine.

PATRICK Still finding it too easy?

HENRY I'm up to A-level stuff now.

PATRICK Wow, all by yourself?

HENRY I have tutors

PATRICK Tut*ors*?

HENRY None of them have been as good as you though.

PATRICK No?

HENRY No, they're much younger, don't know as much, straight from uni mostly. I even corrected my maths tutor the other day: we were doing trigonometrical functions and he was saying that cotan was sine over cosine when it's *obviously* cosine over sine, *idiot*!

PATRICK You have a maths tutor now?

HENRY Yeah.

PATRICK As well?

HENRY Yeah.

PATRICK How many do you have?

HENRY A couple. Mum's gone a bit mental.

PATRICK What's all this for?

HENRY Just, end-of-year exams.

PATRICK End-of-year exams? You'll fly through them.

HENRY Mum just wants to make sure.

PATRICK Of what?

HENRY That I'll pass the year.

PATRICK Of course you'll pass the year, Henry, if you're at A-level standard?

HENRY She doesn't know that though.

PATRICK Oh?

HENRY I tell her I'm still struggling, with school stuff.

PATRICK To keep your tutors?

HENRY I give them an extra fiver not to say anything.

PATRICK You give them a…?

HENRY They don't care. It's a drink to them.

PATRICK But she must see your other results, Henry.

HENRY So.

PATRICK So you're hardly fooling her there.

HENRY I'm failing at school.

Beat.

PATRICK What? You can't be serious? Henry… Why? For how long?

HENRY Oh I totally forgot, I got you something. *(goes to his bag)*

PATRICK Is this so you can keep your tutors?

HENRY I hope it's not too wet.

PATRICK Because you should be getting special/ education really.

HENRY *(about the present)* It's not too bad.

As he takes it out, a ticket, unbeknownst to them both, drops to the floor.

PATRICK A guy of your intelligence.

HENRY *(holding out a wrapped package)* My big news.

PATRICK Are you listening to what I'm saying?

HENRY Take your present.

PATRICK You're not even listening to me.

HENRY You're not even taking my present.

PATRICK Henry.

HENRY Patrick.

PATRICK Stop it.

HENRY Stop what?

PATRICK You don't need to do all this, you can get special assistance.

HENRY What if I don't want that though?

PATRICK Why not?

HENRY Because I don't want to be 'special'

PATRICK But/ you are sp..

HENRY Here, shut up, Jesus, just take your stupid present.

__HENRY__ tosses the present at __PATRICK__. A moment.

PATRICK Are you being bullied again?

HENRY I think I might go.

  HENRY *goes to leave.*

PATRICK What? Wait! Henry! OK I'm sorry, I won't say anything, I'm sorry!

  HENRY *stops. A pause.* **PATRICK** *takes up the present.*

PATRICK Thank you for this. It's very kind of you.

  As **PATRICK** *begins unwrapping it, revealing a small gift box,* **HENRY** *begins to speak.*

HENRY I started doing Karate. Mum wanted me to, just in case, you know, after you left, in case…so as that I can *(doing an impression of his annoying Mum)* "stand up for myself in a fight". I enjoy it though, not that I've needed it since but still, I like the discipline, keeps me fit. Plus no one from school's there so I can chill out. Few weeks ago though we were in the middle of a break and (there's four of us who are really good friends) we were just hanging out near one of the studios. It's David Lloyd's. Andrew pulled me aside and said that Becs really liked me and wanted to snog. I looked down the corridor and saw Becs looking up with this grin on her face that I'd never seen on a girl before. I felt like, just felt, scared. The other two pushed me and Becs into one of the disabled toilets, everyone seemed so giddy all of a sudden. I know that guys from school do this with girls from the school across the road but I didn't think *these* guys were like that and that's why I liked them so I suddenly felt so shit and that I was the centre of a joke or something and I now hated these guys for putting me up to this and why couldn't they just see that I didn't bloody want to? We just stood there in the toilet. For ages. I was staring at the wall, looking at her every now and again with her arms crossed, chewing on one of her fake red nails from the side of her mouth and I hated her so much and I thought "who the hell wears fake nails to

Karate?" She asked me if I was gonna, you know, snog, but I'd never done it before so I asked her how. She looked weird at me first but then saw that I was serious and looked at me like I was the most worthless piece of shit in the entire universe. And then she laughed. She laughed so hard. I couldn't speak. I couldn't see. I slowly opened the door. The boys outside started cheering and patting me on my back, but I just went straight past them and got my stuff and I ran home and I went up to my room and lay on the floor and cried. I couldn't stop. I wanted to kill myself.

PATRICK *goes over to* **HENRY** *and consoles him with a hug.* **PATRICK** *then sees the ticket on the ground.*

PATRICK What's this?

HENRY *(thinking he's referring to the container)* A surprise.

PATRICK No, this.

HENRY What?

PATRICK *picks up the ticket.*

HENRY Oh.

PATRICK It's a LUAS ticket.

HENRY Yeah.

PATRICK Dated today.

HENRY I got the tram.

PATRICK I thought your mum gave you a lift.

HENRY She did.

PATRICK Are you lying to me?

HENRY No, she did.

PATRICK You said she dropped you here.

HENRY No, she/ …

PATRICK But she didn't.

HENRY She dropped me *to* the tram.

PATRICK But not to here.

HENRY No.

PATRICK So you did lie to me.

Beat.

HENRY Yes, but/ …

PATRICK Henry.

HENRY I didn't want to worry you.

PATRICK Is your mum even here?

HENRY What?

PATRICK In Ireland?

HENRY Yes, of course.

PATRICK Then why are you lying to me?

HENRY Because.

PATRICK Because what?

HENRY If you knew I was trekking half way across Dublin on my own to come see you, I knew you'd be worried.

PATRICK What?!

HENRY Like now. You are.

PATRICK I don't believe you.

HENRY Why not?

PATRICK Why should I? You've already lied to me.

HENRY (Oh my God).

PATRICK Henry, you know I can't stand…*(coolly)* Where is she then?

HENRY Who? Mum?

PATRICK Yeah, where is she?

HENRY With friends, her Uni friends.

PATRICK Whereabouts?

HENRY I'm not sure. North Dublin somewhere?

PATRICK Surely she said?

HENRY Clon-*tarf*?

PATRICK *(almost sarcastic)* Oh, Clontarf?

HENRY Is that North Dublin?

PATRICK …Yes.

HENRY And yes, actually, now that I think of it, it *was*. Clontarf Castle. Interrogation over? Because if you really don't believe me then fine, I thought there was a whole load more trust between us but clearly not.

PATRICK

HENRY Why won't you to speak to my Mum?

PATRICK

HENRY You two used to get along so well, then nothing. Seems a bit strange doesn't it?

PATRICK As your Mum said people fall out of touch.

HENRY Yeah, over time, not instantly.

PATRICK Well…

HENRY And whenever I talk to her about you now she goes silent and changes the subject.

PATRICK I thought you said she was looking forward to seeing me?

Pause.

HENRY When did you meet?

PATRICK At Brook Green, at the church.

HENRY No, *when* did you meet?

PATRICK Eh, few weeks before I met you, a year ago now actually.

HENRY How?

PATRICK Why are you asking me this?

HENRY I'm just asking, how?

PATRICK At one of the prayer meetings, you know this.

HENRY What was it about?

PATRICK That one in particular?

HENRY Yes.

PATRICK I can't remember exactly, 'Science in the Bible' or something.

HENRY Oh come on, Captain Specificity.

PATRICK Em… Oh, it was about, I was talking about… I was comparing the religious idea of eternity, with entropy, and I remember that now because I got a standing ovation afterwards. *(he smiles at this)* And then your mum came up to me to talk about you.

HENRY Me?

PATRICK Yes, because she knew you were interested in science but couldn't get you to come to mass and that's why she eventually then asked me to come and tutor you.

HENRY Oh. Oh.

PATRICK So I said I would and the next few months were only a pleasure, so… "You were the brightest kid I'd ever met" I told her.

Beat.

HENRY What's 'entrepony'?

PATRICK Huh?

HENRY That thing you just said.

PATRICK Oh, entropy?

HENRY Yeah.

PATRICK It states, it basically states…it's the second law of thermodynamics and it basically says that anything that has an order must, lose that order, become chaos.

HENRY OK…?

PATRICK As in…take this church, say over time it's going to gradually erode and fall apart from wind and rain erosion without any maintenance, and the more it becomes eroded the weaker the structure becomes and so the quicker the erosion occurs on top of that, so the rate of erosion is exponential as well. As in, the longer time goes by, the more likely it is of something ordered becoming chaos. Understand?

HENRY I think so. Was that a metaphor for religion?

PATRICK *didn't intend for it to be but sees* HENRY*'s point.*

HENRY It's funny you know. I mean, ultimately, you failed.

PATRICK I failed?

HENRY Yeah. You failed. I'm sure that's hard for you to hear but I still don't believe in religion, do I? I should get my money back really.

PATRICK Oh should you now?

HENRY Well I still don't get it.

PATRICK Get what?

HENRY You. You're so intelligent and yet you believe in such, nonsense. Why? I mean, you just…you perplex me.

Beat.

PATRICK What's happening to the sun right now?

HENRY Huh?

PATRICK The sun, what's happening to it?

HENRY It's, burning up.

PATRICK Lots of energy, constantly giving it off until eventually what?

HENRY It has no more.

PATRICK Becomes a…?

HENRY A red giant first.

PATRICK Exactly, it's expanded, two hundred and fifty times bigger than now.

HENRY It'll spread past the Earth's orbit, the planets will burn up.

PATRICK And as it slowly cools down it becomes a/…?

HENRY White dwarf.

PATRICK Good man, you've remembered. What next?

HENRY I don't know. You didn't tell me.

PATRICK Well, our Galaxy has about, how many stars?

HENRY 300 Billion.

PATRICK Yes, and then there are billions and billions of other galaxies on top of that, each with their own billions of other stars, and, *eventually* (this is the most likely theory) they'll all burn out, just like ours, they have to, there's nothing else to do. All the planets that supported life no longer will, there'll be no life to be found anywhere, no nothing, no escape, everything that was anything will just be rocks floating about, crashing into each other (though extremely rarely) and gradually over time becoming nothing but degraded photons, and molecules until, that's it, that's all there is out there, and there'll be nothing out there or here for trillions and trillions and trillions of years, forever basically. And if you want to know how big a trillion is (because I don't think people think enough about this kind of thing) a trillion is…say a million seconds/ is…

HENRY 12 days.

PATRICK Yes! And a trillion seconds is/ …

HENRY 31,688 years.

PATRICK Henry, you, are…yes, unbelievable. And that's what, when I read the Bible, those trillions of years, that's the apocalypse. And so *we*, human beings… the amount of time it's possible for the universe to support life, as we know it, now you won't believe this but, it's the merest, measliest fraction you could think of: life, during the universe's lifespan, is only possible for one thousandth, *of* a billion billion billion, billion billion billion, billion billion billionth, of a *percent. (beat)* And to me, that miniscule amount of time worth nothing really, that's God. The only time there can ever be love is when there's life, and that's now. And when I see people on the news, violence, you know? And people killing each other, kids with guns, for dominance or diamonds or whatever, for things that are so insignificant, and I just think to myself, life is too precious. We should be dedicating our lives to loving one another, to finding someone else, someone… someone who's the reason you want to turn the page over just to find out what happens next. *(beat)* Because there's nothing rarer, in the entire universe, than loving someone, and them loving you back.

Beat.

HENRY Do you love someone?

Moment.

PATRICK No.

Long pause.

HENRY It's our anniversary today, isn't it?

PATRICK

HENRY Or, just, the day, we met, a year ago. Sorry, that word was a bit strong.

PATRICK No, no…

Beat.

HENRY *(excited)* Mate, you still haven't opened your present yet! *(goes to get it)*

PATRICK I did.

HENRY No but you didn't look inside it.

PATRICK 'Mate'?

HENRY *(amused at himself)* Sorry. 'Patrick'. (Sorry I don't know where that…) *(handing the gitft box)* here.

PATRICK *takes the gift box, opens it, and takes out a small bottle. His expression goes from smiling to confused to slightly perturbed.*

PATRICK What's this?

HENRY Something which…so you don't feel guilty anymore…in case that's what the problem was?

PATRICK

HENRY I was awake that night.

PATRICK What night?

HENRY Shit.

PATRICK

HENRY Cos I don't want/ you to feel…

PATRICK Henry, what night?

HENRY Just…the night you babysat. *(beat)* We watched 'The Lion King' didn't we? *Your* DVD by the way, hilarious. I thought it was just a kid's film but when you said how it was like a cartoon version of Hamlet, I thought 'all right, give it a go', and you kept making comparisons throughout between the two (which I disagree with now by the way, if Rosencrantz and Guildenstern are meant to be Timon and Pumba? I mean, Hamlet has them sent to be killed, whereas Simba protects them, it's just…there's too many inconsistencies for my liking but anyways). The heatwave, was *so* hot, *all* of the time, and about halfway through I asked if it would bother you if I took off my pyjamas and sat in my underwear. You said it wouldn't…you stopped making comparisons though. *(beat)* The film got so tense (that bit with Scar and Simba over the fire? It was like we were there, in the heat) and I was chewing so hard on my nails by the end. You told me to stop. That it was an awful habit. And that I looked *disgusting*…that was the last you thing you ever said to me actually: to stop biting my nails. Then I went to bed. *(beat)* I'm lying in bed now, no pyjamas, sheets off me, tossing and turning. Feeling so annoyed at myself cos I upset you. "God sake Mum, we're ordering air-conditioning for this house the second you get home from your bloody gala!" I open my window and my door to try and get some air circulating. There's light from the landing but I don't mind. I lie there, sprawled, trying to sleep, for like an hour *(beat)* There're footsteps coming up the stairs. I go still. You're standing in the doorway. I shut my eyes, you think I'm asleep but I'm not. I can hear you breathing. A minute or two goes by. The two of us, just waiting there, still. *(beat)* I hear you move, your belt being undone. You try to do it quietly but I can still hear you. Your button's undone, and your zip goes down, and then your trousers a bit as well. I open my eyes slightly, you can't see them though cos of the angle, it's darker my side of the room. *(beat)* You take out your…it's [big]. I've never seen one like that in real life before. You begin to shake it, vigorously, just these short, sharp movements, and your entire body's rigid, your face is just staring at me, blank. And I'm just lying there, staring at you, blank. I don't move a muscle. Then your whole body starts to shake, pulsing, randomly, you can't control it, and your breathing, it gets faster. You put out your other hand beneath it, because you're about to…and you do, and when you do you catch it all. In your hand. You slow down. You stop shaking. Your breathing calms and you begin to relax, like you've just finished a big race or something. You squeeze the rest of it out onto your hand. You raise it up to your mouth, and eat it, tossing it back like a tablet, licking your palm. I hear the front door open. Suddenly you're all panicked, like you've just snapped out of a trance. You pull up your trousers, really quickly, you rush out, and go back downstairs. That was the last time I saw you.

Long pause.

PATRICK Where did you get that from?

HENRY What do you mean?

PATRICK Who put you up to that?

HENRY No one did, what/ are you…?

PATRICK Was it your Mum?

HENRY What?

PATRICK Did your Mum put you up to that?

HENRY No!

PATRICK Why are you telling lies?

HENRY I'm not telling/ lies.

PATRICK Henry.

HENRY *You* are.

PATRICK I don't know where you got that story from.

HENRY I got it from nowhere.

PATRICK Then why are you saying this?

HENRY Because I saw you.

Beat.

PATRICK It must have been a dream.

HENRY No it wasn't.

PATRICK It was, Henry, you dreamt it.

HENRY I remember it vividly.

PATRICK There was a heatwave, Henry.

HENRY That doesn't/ mean anything.

PATRICK You must have been hallucinating or something.

HENRY Why are you/…?

PATRICK You were dehydrated.

HENRY I'm not/…

PATRICK And you should have taken a glass of water to bed with you.

HENRY I'm not angry at you Patrick.

PATRICK *I'm* angry at *you.*

HENRY For what?

PATRICK Accusing me of this!

HENRY It's not an accusation.

PATRICK Then what is it?

HENRY *I* can ejaculate now!

PATRICK

HENRY (*pointing to the bottle*) Our bodies are the same now.

> **PATRICK** *holds up the bottle to the light, not quite believing his eyes.*

HENRY Why did you leave? The night you babysat?

PATRICK

HENRY Something happened between you and Mum, I know it. She kept asking me if you'd said anything or done anything to me over and over again and I kept telling her "no" and asking her "what was she talking about?" until she finally left it. She wouldn't let me speak of you ever again.

Pause.

PATRICK Where does she think you are?

Beat.

HENRY At Rupert's.

PATRICK *begins to laugh, slowly at first, then rising hysterically, before falling to nothing.*

HENRY What's so funny?

PATRICK

HENRY We can be together now Patrick.

A moment. **PATRICK** *suddenly looks to the stage right door then back to* **HENRY.**

PATRICK Em…

HENRY What?

PATRICK Are you? Hungry? Have you eaten?

HENRY No.

PATRICK Why don't we, em… there's no food here. Let's grab something, there's a café round the corner.

HENRY OK.

PATRICK It's just by the Post Office.

HENRY Are you all right?

PATRICK Of course, no, I just have to sort something first, I'll catch up. So you go out of here, turn right.

HENRY I know where the Post Office is, I walked past it.

PATRICK Great. Great. Em, here. *(he hands* **HENRY** *his backpack)* You order ahead, I won't be long.

HENRY Cool.

HENRY *goes to leave stage right, but turns in the doorway.*

HENRY You're sure you're all right?

PATRICK Of course. Oh, order me a coffee. Not instant.

HENRY *smiles. Exits.*

Silence. Patrick quickly hides the bottle and gift box. He tris to compose hmself but **NOLEEN** *enters (stage left), startling him.*

NOLEEN Me grandson, Billy was tellin' me the other day there they'll soon be able to tell everythin' about how a baby'll turn out before he's even born. Isn't that mad?

Even the sexual orientation, like. Apparently there's one called 'object' sexuality where people fall in love with inanimate objects. There's a woman married to the Eiffel Tower. That must have been an expensive weddin'.

JACINTA, *clad in her niqab, bounds in through the door (stage right) and catches the end of this.*

JACINTA I'll tell you whose weddin' is goin to be expensive. Eh, mine! *(she holds up a pregnancy test to* **PATRICK***)* Negative!

PATRICK *stares at her.*

JACINTA What's wrong with you?

PATRICK Nothing.

JACINTA Ye sure?

PATRICK Yeah.

JACINTA Don't seem it.

PATRICK So it's negative, the test?

JACINTA Yeah.

PATRICK That's great, em. Sorry, I haven't made the call yet but if you're in a rush you can head off and I'll sort it out.

JACINTA I think I'll wait thanks.

PATRICK Honestly, it's grand.

JACINTA No, you had yer chance. I wanna see you doin' it.

Beat.

PATRICK All right, yeah.

PATRICK *quickly begins looking for his address book.* **JACINTA** *looks around.*

JACINTA How are ye, Noleen?

NOLEEN I'm grand, thanks.

JACINTA Yer keepin' to yerself for once

NOLEEN I am.

PATRICK *is still searching, he can't find it.*

PATRICK (Where'd I put it?)

JACINTA What's up?

NOLEEN Well. I was just thinkin' actually, that you smelt different.

JACINTA *Smell?* Ye can't smell me Noleen

NOLEEN I can. Especially you. There's a strange smell off you, can smell it from miles away, and I was sayin' it to Father just earlier there so I was, wasn't I Father? And I was out there thinkin', there's somethin', there's definitely somethin' about that smell now that I recognise, and do ye know, I've cracked it.

JACINTA Have you?

NOLEEN I have. Congratulations.

JACINTA For wha'?

NOLEEN The new child.

JACINTA What child? There's no child.

NOLEEN There is. I can smell him.

JACINTA takes off the face-veil portion of the niqab.

JACINTA Wha'?

NOLEEN I can smell him in yer belly. Did ye not know?

JACINTA No, I *thought* there might have been one Noleen, but there isn't.

NOLEEN He's still there all right.

JACINTA No he's not.

NOLEEN He is!

JACINTA He isn't! I just did a test and it's negative for God's sake! (I mean Allah).

PATRICK's attention has been drawn to their conversation. JACINTA looks at him.

JACINTA How are ye getting on?

He holds up the address book.

PATRICK Found it.

JACINTA Well?

He dials the number into the phone which is soon answered…

PATRICK Hello, hi Marie?… Father Patrick O'Brien here, Churchtown…yeah. How are ye?… Good, good, em, is the archbishop in?…Great, could I just have a word please?…thanks…

Beat.

NOLEEN What would you have called the baby, Jacinta? Out of curiosity, like.

JACINTA There is no baby, Nolers.

NOLEEN But what if there was? Just in case.

JACINTA Noleen, even if there was a baby, not even God himself would have the power to see it get a name.

NOLEEN What d'ye mean by that?

JACINTA Just…leave it Noleen.

Beat.

NOLEEN Jacinta, love (sorry to be botherin' ye) but would you mind just tellin' me somethin' real quick?

JACINTA *(exasperated)* There isn't no baby, Noleen!

NOLEEN No, it's not to do with the baby this time.

JACINTA What's it to do with then?

NOLEEN The lamp. What's it made of?

JACINTA The lamp?

NOLEEN *(pointing up)* Yeah, on the ceiling there…

JACINTA *(looking up)* Where?

NOLEEN There. Up there somewhere.

JACINTA What's it *made* of?

NOLEEN Yeah.

Beat.

JACINTA I dunno. Brass or somethin'. Why?

NOLEEN Oh, nothin'.

NOLEEN *looks towards* **PATRICK**, *tapping her nose. He registers this, but his attention is suddenly brought back to the phone call.*

PATRICK Hi, Archbishop, yes, em…

He looks back to **JACINTA**.

PATRICK …yeah, no I'm still…*(beat)* I apologise, Archbishop, I'm gonna have to call you back.

He hangs up the phone.

JACINTA What ye do tha' for?

PATRICK Let me see that test.

JACINTA Why?

PATRICK Just let me see it.

JACINTA *(holding it out)* It's negative, see.

Beat.

PATRICK Go back to the chemist and buy another one.

JACINTA The chemist's closed now.

PATRICK Then go tomorrow.

JACINTA I'm flyin' tomorrow.

PATRICK Then go to *another* chemist Jacinta, there's more than one chemist in Dublin! And *then*, bring the test back here. There's a toilet in there which you can use, only this time *I'm* watching you do it.

JACINTA What? Ye bleedin'/ perv.

PATRICK Listen! *If* the reading is negative *that* time round, as you claim it is now, *then* I'll make the call, and you can be on your merry way. But if not then no way, because I know exactly what you'll do to that child if it is. But you shouldn't have to worry about that happening though, should you? Because you're telling the truth. Right?

Pause.

JACINTA I really didn't want to have to do this.

JACINTA *searches through her bag.*

PATRICK Well that's how it's going to be.

JACINTA I was tryin' to protect ye, but ye give me no choice.

She pulls out her phone and clicks through to her emails.

PATRICK What are you up to now?

JACINTA Ye just couldn'ta left it. And now Noleen'll be here to hear all this.

PATRICK Hear what?

JACINTA "Dear Jacinta" *(she looks up to Patrick, then back to her phone)* "I am pleased you have written to me in advance of approaching Father Patrick O'Brien. However, it distresses me greatly to inform you he is not a man to be trusted, especially with your children. Do not be fooled, he is an extremely intelligent person. He can be charming and flirtatious, to the point where he can make you feel special, even loved, but he is also extremely cunning. He will use any means necessary to earn your trust, to gain entry to your house and, ultimately, have access to your children. I am horrified to say I have fallen victim to his manipulations and have placed my son at great risk by leaving him alone in his company. There was an incident of suspected foul-play last year, but my son has since been too traumatised to discuss the situation, yet when I confronted Patrick about it, he was very quickly and very conveniently removed from our Parish and relocated elsewhere, which I now know to be Dublin…"

JACINTA *looks back up to Patrick.*

JACINTA Is that enough? Or do want to hear more from 'Mrs E. Carter'?

Pause. The priest remains still.

PATRICK Evelyn.

JACINTA What?

PATRICK Her name's Evelyn Carter. *(beat)* She was a Eucharistic Minister at my parish in London. Lovely woman, very involved in the church, but she suffered from a psychological disorder called Pseudologia Fantastica. Everyone knew this and it was manageable at first, but her condition deteriorated. She became emotionally unstable and started conducting these wild/ fantasies about the two of us…

JACINTA No, stop it, yer lying/

PATRICK …being a couple, and being in love, we had to get the/ authorities involved…

JACINTA Yer lying!/ …

PATRICK She doesn't even have a son!

Beat.

JACINTA Yes, she does.

PATRICK No, she doesn't.

JACINTA She/ does!

PATRICK And how *dare* you threaten me with something like this!

JACINTA I didn't want to, you/ forced me to.

PATRICK You'd do anything to get your way, wouldn't you?

JACINTA She's pressing charges.

PATRICK Then where are they? Huh? If she's pressing charges, on something that happened a year ago, why haven't they been pressed yet?

JACINTA

PATRICK You disgust me, you know that? Only ever thinking about yourself, at the expense of others, no matter what the cost.

JACINTA Just make the phone/ call.

PATRICK Get out.

JACINTA Or I'll go to the/ guards

PATRICK Now.

JACINTA Please!

PATRICK Never! I will never allow an innocent child to be murdered!

JACINTA What? No. No, there's nothing you can do to stop me, I'm getting rid of it anyway.

PATRICK You do anything to that child and I will personally phone the sheikh and tell him everything myself.

JACINTA Ye can't do that.

PATRICK Yes I can, you gave me his number!

PATRICK *holds up the piece of paper which* **JACINTA** *gave him earlier.*

JACINTA But…ye wouldn't do tha'?

PATRICK Yes I would.

JACINTA Why?

PATRICK Because it's a person's life!

JACINTA Yeah and it's my life too. Why don't I count?

PATRICK Well you should have thought/ about that before…

JACINTA One happy life is better than two miserable ones.

PATRICK *(referring to the niqab)* And a life covered in that isn't miserable?

JACINTA This isn't misery, it's savin' me.

PATRICK *Saving* you?

JACINTA All new Muslims get their slate wiped clean, did ye know tha'? *(becoming upset)* Did ye? Do you know how glorious that makes me feel inside? To be given a second chance when I was never even given a/ chance in the first place?

PATRICK I'm done talking about this.

JACINTA And you wanna take all that/ away from me?

PATRICK The conversation is over.

JACINTA How can your heart/ be so cold?!

PATRICK There's the door.

JACINTA But/ …

PATRICK *Leave!*

JACINTA, *a broken woman, stares at the exit.*

NOLEEN Jacinta?

JACINTA No, Noleen.

>**JACINTA** *composes herself as she prepares to leave, but just as she goes to do so,* **HENRY** *enters stage left.*

HENRY Patrick, I'm worried about you.

>**HENRY** *stops when he sees the now frozen* **PATRICK**, **NOLEEN** *and* **JACINTA** *all staring at him.*

HENRY *(holding out his hand to* **JACINTA***)* Hi, I don't believe/ we've met.

PATRICK Hen…stop…don't.

HENRY Don't what?

JACINTA Eh, where'd you come from?

HENRY London.

PATRICK Henry.

HENRY What?

JACINTA London?

HENRY Yeah.

PATRICK Stop.

Beat.

JACINTA What's goin' on here?

PATRICK Nothing.

JACINTA *(to* **HENRY***)* Henry? His name's Henry? What's goin' on here?

PATRICK Henry/ don't answer that.

HENRY Carter.

JACINTA Carter?!

PATRICK Henry!

HENRY Yeah.

Beat.

JACINTA Then yer ma's Mrs E. Carter?

PATRICK *Don't* answer that Henry.

>**HENRY** *looks between* **PATRICK** *and* **JACINTA**.

JACINTA Jesus Christ what the hell is goin' on here?

PATRICK You're not to say another word, OK?

HENRY *nods.*

JACINTA *(to Henry)* Yer real. *(to Patrick)* And you're silencin' the kid?

PATRICK That's not what/ I'm doing.

JACINTA Ye are! Jesus Christ… *(suddenly, to* **HENRY***)* Does your Ma know you're here? She doesn't, does she?

HENRY

JACINTA Oh my God *(to* **PATRICK***)* Have you kidnapped him? *(to* **HENRY***)* Has he kidnapped you?

PATRICK No one's kidnapped anyone Jacinta. He's safe, he's happy.

JACINTA I don't care. Somethin's not right about this.

PATRICK The only thing that's not right about this is you still being here. I've already expressed my opinion on your situation, and that's that. So if you wouldn't mind I think it's time you leave.

JACINTA Oh I'm leavin' all right. Leavin' to call the guards.

PATRICK Excuse me?

JACINTA You heard me.

> **JACINTA** *goes to leave but she is stopped when* **PATRICK** *calls after her.*

PATRICK You call the guards they're gonna come down here and see that there's nothing suspect going on and you will, yet again, have proven yourself/ an utter nuisance.

JACINTA Oh *enough* o' yer bluffin'! It's all lies!

PATRICK I'm not lying.

JACINTA Ye are! Caught red handed and still denyin' it? How stupid d'ye think I am? I know exactly what I'm talkin' about. And when I show the guards his ma's email they're gonna show up here and see you with her kid? It's not gonna be hard to put one and one together and that'll be it. You'll be done for.

> **PATRICK** *laughs at this.*

JACINTA What?

PATRICK Nothing, nothing. No, yeah, you're right. Go. Go on.

Beat.

JACINTA Don't worry. I'm goin'.

She marches towards the exit, but -

NOLEEN Don't Jacinta, they're happy together!

JACINTA *stops. Slowly, she turns around to look at* **NOLEEN**.

JACINTA What did you just say?

NOLEEN They're happy together.

JACINTA Who?

NOLEEN Father and the boy.

Silence.

NOLEEN *(to* **PATRICK***)* "Were you in love with Brother Kelly? *(beat)* That was my question to Dougie. "Were you in love with Brother Kelly?" *(beat)* "Yes", he said. They were awful to Dougie in that school, Father, the Brothers. Students as well. The beatin's and abuse. He'd been puttin' up with it for years. His soul was broke. Until Brother Kelly. We can find refuge in the strangest of places, Father. I don't fully comprehend it meself but sure then who am I? I try me best and I say me prayers, and there's so much I don't understand. But the night terrors that Dougie suffered all his life from walkin' in and findin' his only, *friend*, in the entire world strung up from his neck like tha'. There was more goin' on than I ever dared ask. I was scared o'course, but Dougie was the gentlest soul I ever met in me life, I thank the Lord every day for sendin' him my way. But now part o'me can't stop wonderin' how happy would they have been if the world just left them alone? *(her voice begins to crack)* And when this young lad called up the church. I was in the community centre one evenin' few weeks back on me own, waitin' for Marina to pick me up. He told me all about you on the phone. Said he'd been tryin' to track you down for weeks, and what you meant to him. Instantly I recognised it. So I told him all too. Where to come. How to get here. That he could stay with me if he liked. *(near tears)* And that's me confession Father. This.

She breaks down crying and falls into **PATRICK**.

PATRICK The heating's been on too long, I think it would be best if we/ took you outside….

NOLEEN And Mary wanted me to see ye today.

PATRICK You're talking nonsense now/ Noleen.

NOLEEN Our Mother, she did. She didn't want me seein' those 'confession's cancelled' signs down the front of the church. She wanted me to come in here, and to smell that *(pointing to the prie-dieu) thing*, and to stop ye, what you were goin' to do to yerself, like Brother Kelly. *Now* I know why she did this *(pointing to her eyes)* to me, Father. To save you.

Long pause..

JACINTA Is that true, Noleen?

PATRICK Of course it's/ not true.

JACINTA *(to* **PATRICK***)* And you held my kid's hand?

PATRICK That's/ …

JACINTA And gave him money to shut him up? You scumbag. You dirty scumbag.

NOLEEN But it's not dirty Jacinta, it's pure.

JACINTA Jesus Noleen, would ye listen to yerself? Can ye even hear what yer sayin'?

HENRY She's right.

Beat.

JACINTA Excuse me?

HENRY I wanted to be here. I came by myself. Patrick didn't know.

JACINTA *(to* **PATRICK***)* So you've indoctrinated the kid, have ye?

HENRY I'm not indoctrinated.

JACINTA Ye are, yer 10.

HENRY I'm not,/ I'm nearly 13.

PATRICK Henry.

JACINTA Ha!

HENRY And he's never done anything to hurt me ever.

*****JACINTA** looks to **PATRICK** who now has no response. She then scans the room and laughs in utter disbelief.*

JACINTA I don't believe this. *(Pause. To **PATRICK**)* All right. All right. Tell ye what. Seems like we've two options here: Option A: You don't make that phone call, *but*, I go straight to the guards right now and tell them everything: about the email, the boy, all that I've seen here today, and we both go about the rest of our lives in absolute misery. *Or.* Option B: You *do* make that phone call, and gimme back my life. Let me go be happy and I'll say nothin'. I'll be outta yer hair. And we all live happily ever after.

*****PATRICK** thinks on this, but his head begins to shake.*

PATRICK No…no…

JACINTA Are you serious?

PATRICK I can't let you do that.

JACINTA So I'm goin' to the guards then? That's what ye want?

HENRY Why can't you just make the phone call, Patrick?

PATRICK Henry/ *please*.

JACINTA *(rubbing her stomach)* Because he's protectin' the unborn.

PATRICK Just let me handle this, OK?

HENRY But then she said she'd leave.

PATRICK Let me *handle* this, Henry.

NOLEEN Can everyone stop?

PATRICK Henry, will you please take Noleen outside?

HENRY I'm not going anywhere.

JACINTA Noleen, go wait in the car.

PATRICK If you disobey me/ once more, Henry.

NOLEEN Why don't we just go, Jacinta?

HENRY You'll what? I'm not/ a child, Patrick.

JACINTA I'm not leavin' here Noleen!

PATRICK You *are* a child!

JACINTA Not until he/ phones.

HENRY No *you're* the child, it's just a bloody abortion!

Beat.

HENRY If it's just an abortion.

PATRICK It's not/ just an…

JACINTA It *is* just an abortion.

HENRY Then let her do it.

JACINTA I don't believe this.

HENRY This is such/ a stupid argument.

JACINTA The kid's on my side.

PATRICK Henry.

HENRY I can't believe we're even having it.

PATRICK Stay out of it.

JACINTA Finally/ *someone* with a bit of compassion around here.

HENRY What? It's just a couple of cells, Patrick, you of all people/ should know that.

JACINTA But ye see, Henry/…

HENRY Just make the call and she'll go away/ and leave us alone.

JACINTA The problem with this endangered breed is -

PATRICK Henry, you don't/ …

HENRY It's none of our/ business anyway.

JACINTA *He* sees things for/ what they *can* be.

PATRICK You don't know what you're talking about.

HENRY Oh don't I?

JACINTA *Not* for what they/ *are*.

PATRICK You're making/ me angry now.

JACINTA Which sounds beautiful in theory.

HENRY No, I'm not.

JACINTA But it's delusional!

HENRY You make your*self* angry, Patrick!

Pause.

HENRY Just leave her alone.

PATRICK Henry.

HENRY It isn't any/ of our…

PATRICK *(aggressively) Shut up*!

Pause.

JACINTA No, I don't feel safe, that kid's not safe with you, yer a lunatic.

PATRICK And you! Get out!

JACINTA Not until you make that call.

PATRICK I'm never making that call.

JACINTA Never? Absolutely never?

PATRICK No.

JACINTA Even when your own life's on the line?

PATRICK It's someone else's life.

JACINTA He won't have a life.

PATRICK Yes, he will.

JACINTA In what universe? No, he won't. He'll be miserable like Mark.

PATRICK So be it.

JACINTA And you're happy with that?

PATRICK Yes.

JACINTA You're happy with misery?

PATRICK He'll still be alive.

JACINTA You can see *no* circumstance where this kid wouldn't be better off never bein' alive?

PATRICK No!

JACINTA No? What if he turned out to be you?

Pause.

PATRICK Huh?

JACINTA *What if he turned out to be just, like, you?*

The overlapping dialogue below should be fluid. There are forward slashes to indicate where people interrupt each other but this may change in performance. **JACINTA**'s *dialogue is the anchor, it should be constant. The others try to speak around her, only interjecting when they can. The pace and intensity of everyone's argument should build and build to a climax on* **JACINTA**'s *final line, which should be clearly heard.*

JACINTA A life like yours. Go on, look at yerself (**JACINTA** *rubs her stomach*) Look at yerself! How could ye live knowin' there was another you in the world: walkin' around, lookin' at kids, thinkin'/ the same dirty thoughts?

PATRICK *(staring at* **JACINTA**'s *stomach)* I don't look at kids like that/

JACINTA Oh but ye do and ye have, I'm sure/ of it, look at ye.

PATRICK I've never done that.

JACINTA And here come the lies, what's tha' like by the way? Lying all the time?

PATRICK I'm not lying.

JACINTA To yerself and everyone else. Lies and lies/ and nothin' but lies.

HENRY Leave him alone.

JACINTA That's all you are, isn't it? One big lie after/ the next. That's not a life, is it?

HENRY Patrick, don't listen to her.

JACINTA No it's pathetic, but ye never/ asked to be like tha, did ye?

NOLEEN Stop it now Jacinta, I/ think we should go.

JACINTA To have a life crippling disease? Cos that's what it is, a disease/

HENRY It's not a disease/ you don't know him at all.

JACINTA A disease that you fight/ but never defeat.

PATRICK Stop it./ Stop it.

JACINTA Ye try/ to control it but ye can't.

NOLEEN Jacinta, darlin', please,/ I want to go home.

JACINTA It takes over yer body,/ its power's too great.

HENRY He told you to stop./ Don't listen to her Patrick, none of it's true.

JACINTA And yer loggin' onto sites, jackin' off over kids,/ but that's not enough.

NOLEEN Jacinta, no, don't be/ talkin' like tha'.

JACINTA So ye earn a child's trust,/ ye get him in close.

PATRICK You don't…/ you don't know the first thing.

JACINTA Ye think "just this/ one time, I'll definitely get away with it".

HENRY Stop listening to her. Patrick, /look at me. Look at me.

JACINTA But yer not thinkin' anymore/ cos yer an animal now.

NOLEEN Don't listen to her, Father.

PATRICK That's not/ …That's not…No. No. Stop.

JACINTA The build up of pleasure, it feels/ fuckin' glorious.

HENRY No. No. Stop it./ He's not like that.

JACINTA You've been dormant too long,/ ye could die from the bliss.

NOLEEN She doesn't understand/ what she's talkin' about.

JACINTA The/ eruption is comin' and the ecstasy peaks!

HENRY You don't know the first thing about him/

JACINTA But as soon as it happens/ yer just back to the start.

HENRY He's the kindest,/ smartest, gentlest, funniest man in the world.

JACINTA It's the murder of innocence, the terrified child.

NOLEEN / She's only young and needs guidance… Guidance, Father.

JACINTA "What the fuck have I done?" But there's nothing/ ye can do.

HENRY He'd never/ do anything to hurt anyone.

JACINTA No means of/ escape, it's a torturous, never-endin' cycle.

NOLEEN We all need guidance from the Lord, Our God.

JACINTA And/ ye constantly keep askin' yerself over and over again.

HENRY He's the only reason I'm alive.

JACINTA DID YE EVER FUCKIN' WANT TO BE BORN IN THE FIRST PLACE?!?!

> *PATRICK's eyes, now transfixed on JACINTA's stomach, are filled with utter hatred. He is unable to control his violently shaking body. As soon as JACINTA finishes speaking, PATRICK lets out a cacophonous, resounding "NO!" and flies a thudding punch into her stomach, keeling her over in agonizing, noiseless pain. HENRY recoils in shock, frozen. NOLEEN whimpers, shaking her head. PATRICK breathes loudly. Suddenly, a screeching howl escapes JACINTA's gut like a ferocious shockwave. It reverberates round the room before slowly dying down. Silence. Another wave of howling loudly continues. NOLEEN begins wailing, slowly walking with her hands out towards JACINTA on the floor, terrified of what she might find. JACINTA continues cluctching her stomach, screaming in pain. HENRY can't take his eyes off her. Throughout the following, PATRICK calmly walks to the pire-dieu, opens it and looks inside. No one else notices him.*

NOLEEN *(speaking/wailing uninterruptedly)* Jacinta! Jacinta! Me darlin' Jacinta! Sacred Heart!/ Jacinta! No! No! The baby!

HENRY Oh my God, oh my God, oh my God.

NOLEEN He's dead. He's dead!/ What have ye done?

HENRY An ambulance. Jesus, she needs an ambulance!

HENRY takes out his phone and tries to calm himself down.

JACINTA *(among her howling)* Help me! Help me! *(etc.)*

NOLEEN is rocking back and forth over JACINTA's body.

NOLEEN The poor baby, ah the/ poor little dead baby.

HENRY What's the number here? Is it the same as at home?

NOLEEN God bless us! What are we doin' to ourselves?

HENRY I don't have any signal. Fuck. Fuck!

NOLEEN Mary, Mary! What's/ the point of it all?

HENRY *(searching)* Landline! Where's the landline?

NOLEEN Holy Mary, mother of God, save our souls!

JACINTA's screams are dying down. She is clutching her stomach.

NOLEEN is shaking, hugging Jacinta tight.

PATRICK has takten out the gun from the prie-dieu.

HENRY turns to see PATRICK who looks to heaven.

He notices the gun in PATRICK's hand.

He is about to lift it to his head.

PATRICK Forgive me, Father/

HENRY Patrick…

PATRICK turns to HENRY.

The room falls silent

Time slows down

We focus on them

Breathing as one

Alone, together

At peace

Calm.

But

What seems like an eternity

Is only a few seconds.

Serenely

PATRICK's *hand,*

As if by a mind of its own,

Has placed the gun in his mouth.

But almost as soon as we notice this -

Bang

End of Play

NOTE

In 2000, The Commission to Inquire into Child Abuse (more commonly known as the Ryan Report) was set up by the Irish government to investigate the extent of child abuse in institutions for children in Ireland from 1936 onwards. It published its findings in 2009. Below is a quote, taken from this report, which was the original inspiration for the play:

> "... I had sexual relations with him. That is the way I look at it. I will say the others abused me, but with him I would be kinder with the words because the man did look after me, but I did do things with him that today people would stand up and scream about. But he was kind. He was probably the only person in my life up to that time. Probably the only person in my life up to that time that would give me a hug, look after me. Anyone, nobody could get to me. You know, he kept the others away. Monitors never reported me because they knew I would report them. Simple. He looked after me, I looked after him. As simple as that ... sexual abuse did take place. But at that time that was mine, I now know that it was wrong. But at the time, if he had asked me to eat his head, I would have eaten his head, as simple as that...he was probably the one person I loved at that point. I did love the man, you know. I know he done that, but I loved him. I have very fond memories of the man. But now I am 68."

A man who was at St Joseph's Industrial School, Artane, in the 1940s.

enry arrives – twelve years old and on a own.

?atrick ever find peace?

>mic but uncompromisingly savage, *Be* ·il is an outstanding debut that complicates modern Ireland, just when we thought we ured out.

o see the truth you must be blinded is false around you..."

n is a native of Dublin now resident in is a trained actor and studied playwriting Carr. He has been a participant of the Royal g Writers' Programme and their Studio

L FRENCH
ers and
resentatives
ch-london.co.uk

ISBN 978-0-573-11488-5

BE INFANTS IN EVIL

SAMUEL FRENCH